Ethixtech Chronicles

Programming Book

Epigraph by ETHIXTECH CHRONICLES:

"In the realm of code and algorithms, let our keystrokes echo the principles of ethics. As we decode the digital language, may our exploration be guided by the compass of responsibility, innovation, and a commitment to a future where technology serves humanity with integrity."

— ETHIXTECH CHRONICLES

Ethixtech   Chronicles

Contents

1.

2.

3.

4.

5.

6.

7.

8.

9.

10.

11.

12.

13.

14.

15.

16.

17.

18.

19.

20.

21.

22.

23.

24.

25.

26.

27.

28.

29.

Foreword

Foreword by ETHIXTECH CHRONICLES:

In the fast-paced corridors of technology, where innovation is the currency and code is the language, "Decoding the Digital Realm" stands as a beacon, illuminating the path for both seasoned technophiles and curious minds alike. In this digital odyssey, we are privileged to witness the marriage of art and logic, where each line of code tells a story and every algorithm whispers the promise of a new frontier.

ETHIXTECH CHRONICLES is thrilled to endorse this captivating journey through the intricate layers of computer instruction processing. As stewards of ethical tech exploration, we believe in the power of knowledge to shape a responsible and enlightened digital future. "Decoding the Digital Realm" aligns seamlessly with our ethos, inviting readers to not only understand the mechanics of programming but to appreciate the ethical considerations that underscore this dynamic field.

As technology continues its relentless march forward, the need for comprehension, ethical discernment, and continuous learning becomes paramount. This book, penned with eloquence and expertise, serves as an invaluable guide. It doesn't just teach; it inspires, urging us to reflect on the ethical implications of our digital endeavors.

In the pages that follow, ETHIXTECH CHRONICLES invites you to embrace the wonders of computer instruction processing. This book is not merely an exploration of code; it is a call to action, an invitation to think critically, and a reminder that the digital realm is not just a space of endless possibilities but a canvas where ethical choices shape the world we inhabit.

With great excitement, we present "Decoding the Digital Realm" by ETHIXTECH CHRONICLES – a journey that promises to elevate your understanding of programming while empowering you to navigate the digital landscape responsibly. Happy reading, and may your exploration of the digital realm be as enlightening as it is exhilarating.

Preface

Preface:

Welcome to the captivating journey through the realm of programming, where the magic of computer instruction processing unfolds. In "Decoding the Digital Realm," we embark on an exploration of the intricate dance between human intent and the silicon heart of our technological landscape.

As we dive into the intricacies of code execution, this journey goes beyond the syntax and algorithms, delving into the very essence of how our instructions transform into digital actions. It's a tale of zeros and ones, of logic and creativity seamlessly intertwined to breathe life into the digital world.

In this book, we unravel the secrets of computer instruction processing – a symphony of electrical pulses, logic gates, and countless lines of code that shape our technological reality. Whether you're a seasoned developer, a curious enthusiast, or someone stepping into the vast universe of programming for the first time, prepare to be enchanted by the beauty and complexity of the processes that power our digital lives.

Together, let's venture into the heart of programming's core, where each line of code is a brushstroke on the canvas of innovation, and every algorithm is a step forward in our collective journey to decode the possibilities of the digital age. Join me as we navigate this thrilling landscape, where curiosity is our compass, learning is our guide, and the language of computers becomes a symphony waiting to be conducted.

Fasten your seatbelt and get ready to embark on an odyssey through the world of computer instruction processing – a journey that promises not just knowledge but a profound understanding of the invisible forces shaping the technological tapestry around us.

Acknowledgement

Acknowledgment by ETHIXTECH CHRONICLES:

In the ever-evolving landscape of technology, where innovation is both a beacon and a challenge, we extend our deepest gratitude to the creators of "Decoding the Digital Realm." Crafting a masterpiece that demystifies the intricacies of computer instruction processing requires not only technical prowess but a profound dedication to ethical exploration.

ETHIXTECH CHRONICLES is honored to acknowledge the brilliant minds behind this enlightening journey. To the authors, whose dedication to excellence shines through each chapter, thank you for illuminating the path for aspiring technologists and seasoned professionals alike. Your commitment to fostering a holistic understanding of programming, coupled with ethical considerations, is commendable.

To the readers embarking on this voyage, know that you are in the capable hands of visionaries who recognize the importance of ethical tech exploration. "Decoding the Digital Realm" is not just a book; it's a testament to the symbiotic relationship between technological advancement and ethical responsibility.

As we celebrate the launch of this remarkable work, let us collectively embrace the ethos embedded in its pages. May your journey through the digital realm be not only educational but also a catalyst for ethical contemplation and responsible innovation.

With sincere appreciation,

ETHIXTECH   CHRONICLES

2. **Choose a Programming Language:**

Choosing the right programming language is a crucial decision that depends on your goals, preferences, and the type of projects you want to work on. Here's a comprehensive guide to help you make an informed choice.

2.1 Understand Your Goals:

- **Web Development:**
    - If you're interested in building websites, consider languages like **HTML, CSS, JavaScript** for front-end, and **Node.js, Python, Ruby on Rails, or PHP** for back-end.

- **Mobile App Development:**
    - For Android apps, learn **Java or Kotlin**, and for iOS apps, learn **Swift**.

- **Data Science and Machine Learning:**
    - **Python** is widely used for data analysis, machine learning, and artificial intelligence due to its rich ecosystem of libraries like NumPy, Pandas, and TensorFlow.

- **General-Purpose and Object-Oriented Programming:**
    - **Python, Java, C++, or C#** are versatile choices for various applications.

- **Scripting and Automation:**
    - For scripting tasks and automation, consider **Python, Ruby, or Bash**.

- **Embedded Systems and Internet of Things (IoT):**
    - Languages like **C or C++** are commonly used for programming embedded systems.

- **Game Development:**
    - **C++ with Unreal Engine or C# with Unity** are popular choices for game development.

2.2 Research Popularity and Community Support:

- **Community Support:**
    - A strong community can be a valuable resource for learning and problem-solving. Languages like **Python and JavaScript** have large and active communities.

- **Job Market:**
    - Consider the demand for specific languages in the job market. **JavaScript, Python, and Java** are often in high demand.

2.3 Consider Learning Curve:

- **Beginner-Friendly:**
    - If you're new to programming, opt for languages with simpler syntax, such as **Python or JavaScript**.

- **Steep Learning Curve:**
    - Some languages, like **C++ or Rust**, have steeper learning curves but offer high performance and control.

2.4 Explore Ecosystem and Libraries:

- **Ecosystem:**
    - Look into the ecosystem of the language. For instance, **Python** has a vast library ecosystem for various applications.

- **Frameworks:**
    - Many languages have frameworks that simplify development. For web development, consider **Django (Python), Flask (Python), Ruby on Rails (Ruby), or Express.js (JavaScript)**.

2.5 Job-Specific Requirements:

- **Industry Standards:**
    - Research industry standards for the field you're interested in. Some sectors have specific language preferences.

- **Company Requirements:**
    - If you have a specific company or job in mind, check their technology stack and preferred languages.

2.6 Learning Resources:

- **Documentation:**
    - Check the official documentation for the language. Well-maintained documentation is a sign of a mature language.

- **Tutorials and Courses:**
    - Explore online tutorials and courses for the language you're considering. Platforms like **Coursera, Udacity, and freeCodeCamp** offer excellent resources.

2.7 Hands-On Practice:

- **Create a Simple Project:**
    - Once you've chosen a language, start a small project to apply what you've learned. It could be a personal website, a simple game, or a script for automating a task.

- **GitHub:**
    - Consider creating a GitHub account to showcase your projects. It's a valuable platform for collaboration and a portfolio for potential employers.

2.8 Stay Flexible:

- **Be Open to Learning Multiple Languages:**
    - While mastering one language is essential, being open to learning new languages expands your skill set and makes you adaptable.

Remember, there is no one-size-fits-all answer. The best language for you depends on your goals and interests. Don't hesitate to explore and try different languages before committing to one. Happy coding!

1

Learn the Basics

Certainly! Let's delve into the basics of programming.

1. Learn the Basics of Programming:

Programming is like giving instructions to a computer to perform a specific task. Before diving into any programming language, it's crucial to understand some fundamental concepts.

1.1 Variables and Data Types:

- Variables: These are containers for storing data values. Think of them as labeled boxes where you can store information. For example:
```python
age = 25
name = "John"
```

- Data Types: Variables can hold different types of data, such as integers, floating-point numbers, strings (text), boolean (true/false), etc. For instance:
```python
age = 25 # Integer
height = 5.9 # Float
name = "John" # String
is_adult = True # Boolean
```

1.2 Basic Control Structures:

-Conditional Statements (if-else): These allow your program to make decisions based on certain conditions.

```python
age = 18
if age >= 18:
print("You are an adult.")
else:
print("You are a minor.")
```

- Loops (for, while): Loops help you repeat a certain block of code multiple times.

```python
for i in range(5):
print("Iteration:", i)
```

1.3 Functions:

- Functions: These are blocks of reusable code. They take input, process it, and return an output.

```python
def greet(name):
return "Hello, " + name + "!"
```

result = greet("Alice")
print(result)
```

#### 1.4 Input and Output:

- **Input:** Allowing the user to input data into your program.

```python
name = input("Enter your name: ")
```
```

```
print("Hello, " + name + "!")
```


- Output: Displaying information to the user.
```python
print("This is an output statement.")
```


1.5 Comments:

- Comments: Adding comments to your code helps explain what it does. These are not executed and are for human readability.
```python
# This is a single-line comment
"""
This is a multi-line comment
spanning multiple lines.
"""
```


1.6 Debugging:

- Debugging:Learning how to identify and fix errors in your code is a crucial skill.
```python
# Example of a common error
age = input("Enter your age: ")
print("You are " + age + " years old.")
```

Here, the `input()` function returns a string, so you might encounter unexpected behavior when trying to perform numerical operations.

1.7 Recommended Resources:

- Online platforms like Codecademy, Khan Academy, and W3Schools offer interactive courses.

Books such as "Python Crash Course" by Eric Matthes or "JavaScript: The Good Parts" by Douglas Crockford provide in-depth learning.

1.8 Practice, Practice, Practice:

-The more you code, the more comfortable you'll become. Use coding platforms like HackerRank or LeetCode for hands-on practice.

Remember, the basics are the foundation of your programming journey. Once you grasp these concepts, you'll find it easier to explore more advanced topics and languages.   Happy   coding!

2

Online Courses

Online Courses:

Enrolling in online courses is an excellent way to structure your learning and gain comprehensive knowledge in programming. Here's a detailed guide on how to make the most of online courses.

1 Choose the Right Platform:

- Coursera:

- Offers courses from universities and organizations worldwide. Specializations and degrees are also available.

- edX:

Similar to Coursera, edX provides courses from universities and institutions. Offers MicroMasters and Professional Certificate programs.

- Udacity:

Focuses on tech-related courses and nanodegree programs. Practical projects are a key component.

Udemy:

Features a wide range of courses on various topics. Often more affordable and accessible.

2 Selecting Courses:

-Beginner-Friendly Courses:

- Start with courses designed for beginners. Look for titles like "Introduction to Programming" or "Programming for Absolute Beginners."

-Structured Learning Paths:

- Opt for courses that provide a structured path, covering fundamental to advanced topics. Specializations or nanodegree programs are great for this.

-Read Reviews:

- Check reviews and testimonials for courses. This can give insights into the course content and effectiveness.

3 Supplement with Practice:

-Hands-On Coding:

- Don't just watch lectures; actively code along. Practical experience is crucial for understanding concepts.

- Coding Challenges:

- Use platforms like HackerRank, LeetCode, or CodeSignal to apply what you've learned in real coding challenges.

4 Time Management:

-Set a Schedule:

- Plan a consistent study schedule. Allocate specific times for lectures, coding practice, and reviewing concepts.

-Break Down Modules:

- If the course is divided into modules, break down your learning into manageable chunks. This helps in better retention.

5 Seek Community Support:

-Discussion Forums:

- Many online course platforms have discussion forums. Engage with other learners, ask questions, and participate in discussions.

- Social Media Groups:

- Join programming communities on platforms like Reddit or Facebook. Share your progress and seek advice.

6 Complete Assignments and Projects:

- Assignments:

- Take assignments seriously. They reinforce your understanding of the material.

-Capstone Projects:

- If the course includes a final project, treat it as an opportunity to showcase your skills. It can also be added to your portfolio.

7 Explore Additional Resources:

-Documentation:

- Supplement your learning with official documentation for the programming language or technology you're studying.

-Books and Blogs:

- Read additional books or follow programming blogs to gain diverse perspectives and insights.

8 Certification and Recognition:

-Certificates:

- While certificates are valuable, prioritize gaining practical skills over collecting certificates. Focus on understanding and applying concepts.

-LinkedIn and Resume:

- Add completed courses to your LinkedIn profile or resume. It demonstrates your commitment to continuous learning.

9 Continuous Learning:

- Stay Updated:

- Programming languages and technologies evolve. Stay updated with the latest industry trends and advancements.

- Advanced Courses:

- Once you have a solid foundation, explore more advanced courses in your area of interest.

10 Reflect and Iterate:

- Reflect on Progress:

- Periodically reflect on your progress. Identify areas where you need more practice or understanding.

-Iterate Your Learning Plan:

- Adjust your learning plan based on your reflections. This ensures a continuous improvement in your programming skills.

Online courses provide a structured and accessible way to learn programming. Combining these courses with practical coding, community engagement, and continuous learning will enhance your programming journey. Happy coding!

3

Books

Books for Learning Programming:

Books are timeless resources that offer in-depth knowledge and structured learning paths. Here's a comprehensive guide on how to make the most of programming books.

1 Choosing the Right Books:

-Beginner-Friendly Titles:

- Start with books tailored for beginners. Look for titles that provide a gentle introduction to programming concepts.

-Language-Specific Books:

- If you've chosen a programming language, find books dedicated to that language. For example, "Python Crash Course" for Python or "Eloquent JavaScript" for JavaScript.

- Project-Oriented Books:

- Consider books that guide you through building projects. Practical application reinforces theoretical knowledge.

2 Reading Strategies:

-Active Reading:

- Read actively by taking notes, highlighting key concepts, and writing summaries. This helps in better retention.

- Code Along:

- Code along with examples in the book. Hands-on coding is crucial for understanding programming concepts.

-Practical Exercises:

- Complete exercises and challenges provided in the book. Apply what you learn through practical work.

3 Supplement with Online Resources:

- Documentation:

- Use official documentation alongside books. It provides real-world usage and additional details.

- Interactive Platforms:

- Practice on interactive platforms like Codecademy or freeCodeCamp to reinforce book concepts.

4 Building a Library:

-Diversify Topics:

- Build a library that covers a range of topics, from language fundamentals to advanced topics like algorithms, data structures, and design patterns.

-Reference Books:

- Have reference books for the languages you use. These can be handy for quick look-ups.

5 Recommended Books for Beginners:

-"Python Crash Course" by Eric Matthes:

- An excellent choice for beginners learning Python through practical projects.

- "JavaScript: The Good Parts" by Douglas Crockford:

- Focuses on the core, good parts of JavaScript, making it a concise and insightful read.

- "Head First Java" by Kathy Sierra and Bert Bates:

- Known for its engaging style, this book is great for those starting with Java.

6 Books for Advanced Topics:

- "Clean Code: A Handbook of Agile Software Craftsmanship" by Robert C. Martin:

- Teaches principles and practices for writing clean, maintainable code.

- "Design Patterns: Elements of Reusable Object-Oriented Software" by Erich Gamma, Richard Helm, Ralph Johnson, and John Vlissides:

- A classic that introduces essential design patterns in software development.

7 Utilizing eBooks and Digital Platforms:

-eBooks and Kindle Versions:

- Consider digital versions for portability and ease of access.

- Interactive Coding Platforms:

- Some books come with interactive coding platforms or companion websites. Take advantage of these resources.

8 Joining Book Clubs or Discussion Groups:

-Community Engagement:

- Join book clubs or online discussion groups focused on programming books. It provides a platform to discuss concepts and gain different perspectives.

9 Continuous Learning:

- Stay Updated:

- Programming evolves. Stay updated with the latest editions of relevant books or explore new titles.

-Explore Specialized Topics:

- As you advance, explore specialized topics such as machine learning, cybersecurity, or game development through dedicated books.

10 Reflect and Apply:

- Apply Knowledge:

- Regularly apply what you learn from books in practical projects. This reinforces understanding.

- Reflection:

- Reflect on how the concepts from books apply to real-world scenarios. This critical thinking enhances your problem-solving skills.

Books are valuable companions in your programming journey. Whether you're a beginner or an experienced developer, a well-curated collection of books can serve as a reference and guide you through various stages of your programming career.   Happy   reading   and   coding!

4

Practice Regularly

Practice Regularly:

Consistent and intentional practice is a cornerstone of becoming proficient in programming. Here's a detailed guide on how to structure and optimize your practice sessions.

1 Set Clear Goals:

- Define Objectives:

- Clearly define what you want to achieve. It could be mastering a specific programming concept, solving a set of coding challenges, or building a small project.

- Long-Term and Short-Term Goals:

- Establish both long-term goals (e.g., building a portfolio) and short-term goals (e.g., mastering a specific algorithm).

2 Structured Learning:

- Follow a Curriculum:

- If you're learning a new language or technology, follow a structured curriculum. This ensures you cover all the essential topics.

- Practice Each Concept:

- After learning a new concept, immediately practice it. This reinforces your understanding.

3 Coding Challenges:

- Use Online Platforms:

- Platforms like LeetCode, HackerRank, and CodeSignal offer a variety of coding challenges. Start with easy ones and gradually progress.

- Focus on Problem Solving:

- Emphasize problem-solving over speed. Understand the problem, plan your solution, and then code.

4 Project-Based Learning:

- Choose Projects Wisely:

- Undertake projects that align with your interests and learning objectives. This could be a personal website, a small application, or a game.

- Break Down Projects:

- Break down larger projects into smaller, manageable tasks. This prevents feeling overwhelmed.

5 Debugging Practice:

- Intentional Bugs:

- Introduce intentional bugs into your code and practice debugging. This sharpens your troubleshooting skills.

- Learn from Mistakes:

- Mistakes are a natural part of coding. Analyze and learn from your errors to avoid repeating them.

6 Time Management:

-Set Aside Dedicated Time:

- Allocate specific times in your schedule for practice. Consistency is more important than the amount of time spent.

- Balanced Practice:

- Balance between learning new concepts, solving challenges, and working on projects. This provides a holistic learning experience.

7 Collaborative Practice:

- Pair Programming:

- Engage in pair programming with a friend or a fellow learner. It exposes you to different perspectives and improves communication skills.

- Code Reviews:

- Participate in or conduct code reviews. Providing and receiving feedback is invaluable for growth.

8 Tools and Environments:

- Use IDEs Effectively:

- Familiarize yourself with Integrated Development Environments (IDEs) relevant to your language. They often include helpful features for coding and debugging.

- Version Control:

- Learn version control systems like Git. It facilitates collaboration and helps manage code changes.

9 Join Coding Communities:

- Online Forums:

- Join forums like Stack Overflow or community platforms related to your programming language. Contribute and learn from others.

- Local Meetups:

- Attend local coding meetups or join online coding groups. Networking with peers enhances your learning experience.

10 Reflect and Iterate:

- Reflect on Progress:

- Regularly reflect on your coding journey. Celebrate achievements and identify areas for improvement.

- Iterate Your Learning Plan:

- Adjust your learning plan based on your reflections. Adapt and focus on areas that need strengthening.

11 Burnout Prevention:

- Take Breaks:

- Avoid burnout by taking breaks. Short breaks during study sessions and longer breaks between intense learning periods are essential.

- Diversify Activities:

- Engage in other activities to maintain a balance. Physical exercise, reading, or hobbies can refresh your mind.

Remember, the key to improvement in programming is consistent and deliberate practice. Approach it with a growth mindset, embracing challenges as opportunities to learn and grow. Happy coding!

5

Join Coding Communities

Join Coding Communities:

Being part of coding communities is an excellent way to enhance your programming journey. Here's a comprehensive guide on how to effectively engage in coding communities.

Choose the Right Communities:

- Programming Languages:

- Join communities focused on the programming languages you are learning or using. For example, Python communities, JavaScript communities, etc.

- Specialized Communities:

- Explore communities related to specific interests, such as web development, machine learning, or game development.

- General Coding Communities:

- Platforms like Stack Overflow, Reddit's r/learnprogramming, or Dev.to offer general programming discussions.

2 Lurk and Learn:

- Observe First:

- When you join a community, take some time to observe discussions and interactions. Learn about community norms and culture.

- Read Documentation:

- Familiarize yourself with community guidelines and rules. Most communities have specific guidelines for posting and interacting.

3 Active Participation:

- Ask Questions:

- Don't hesitate to ask questions when you're stuck. However, ensure you've done some research on your own first.

- Answer Questions:

- Contribute by answering questions within your knowledge range. Teaching others reinforces your own understanding.

4 Share Your Progress:

- Showcase Projects:

- Share your coding projects with the community. It could be a small script, a website, or a game. This opens opportunities for feedback.

- Write About Your Journey:

- Consider writing blog posts or making social media updates about your programming journey. It can inspire others and provide a sense of accountability.

5 Attend Meetups and Events:

- Local Meetups:

- Attend local coding meetups if possible. They provide an excellent opportunity to network with professionals and enthusiasts.

- Online Events:

- Participate in webinars, virtual conferences, or live coding sessions. These events often feature experienced developers sharing their knowledge.

6 Collaborate on Projects:

- Open Source Contributions:

- Contribute to open-source projects. It's a fantastic way to collaborate with others and gain real-world coding experience.

- Join Hackathons:

- Participate in hackathons or coding challenges hosted by the community. They encourage creativity and problem-solving.

7 Be Respectful and Constructive:

- Positive Interaction:

- Maintain a positive and respectful tone in your interactions. Constructive feedback is appreciated, but negativity is discouraged.

- Handle Criticism Gracefully:

- If you receive criticism, view it as an opportunity for improvement. Respond gracefully and use it as a learning experience.

8 Network and Build Relationships:

- Connect with Peers:

- Build connections with fellow learners and professionals. Networking can lead to valuable insights and opportunities.

- LinkedIn and GitHub:

- Keep your LinkedIn and GitHub profiles updated. These platforms serve as your coding resume.

9 Stay Informed:

- Stay Updated:

- Regularly check community updates, announcements, and relevant news. Staying informed keeps you connected with the community.

- Follow Influencers:

- Follow influential figures in the community on social media. Their insights and updates can be valuable.

10 Be Consistent:

- Consistent Engagement:

- Consistency is key. Regularly engage with the community, whether it's daily, weekly, or according to your schedule.

- Set Boundaries:

- Balance your time in the community with your personal and study time. Avoid burnout by setting boundaries.

Engaging in coding communities is not just about learning; it's about building a network, gaining exposure, and contributing to a larger ecosystem.

32

Approach it with enthusiasm, and you'll find the community to be a powerful resource throughout your programming journey. Happy coding and connecting!

6

Contribute to Open Source

Contribute to Open Source:

Contributing to open-source projects is an enriching way to advance your programming skills. Here's an in-depth guide on how to get started and make meaningful contributions.

1 Understanding Open Source:

- What is Open Source?

- Open-source projects are collaborative initiatives where the source code is accessible to the public. Anyone can view, use, modify, and contribute to the code.

-Benefits of Open Source Contributions:

Enhances your coding skills, provides real-world experience, and allows you to work on impactful projects. It's also an excellent way to build a portfolio.

2 Selecting a Project:

- Find a Project of Interest:

- Choose a project aligned with your interests and skills. GitHub is a popular platform to discover open-source projects.

- Assess Project Documentation:

Check if the project has clear documentation, a contributing guide, and an active community. This ensures a smoother onboarding process.

3 Onboarding and Setup:

Familiarize Yourself:

Read the project's README and contributing guidelines thoroughly. Understand the project's structure, technologies used, and coding conventions.

Set Up the Development Environment:

Follow the setup instructions provided by the project. This may involve installing dependencies, configuring settings, and running the project locally.

4. Start Small:

Begin with Beginner-Friendly Tasks:

Look for issues labeled as "beginner-friendly" or "good first issue." These are usually well-suited for newcomers.

- Fixing Bugs:

Bug fixes are a great starting point. They allow you to understand the codebase and make positive contributions.

5 Effective Communication:

Join the Project's Communication Channels:

Engage with the project's community through communication channels like Slack, Discord, or mailing lists. Introduce yourself and express your interest in contributing.

Ask Questions:

Don't hesitate to ask questions if you're unsure about certain aspects of the project. Open-source communities are generally supportive.

6 Version Control and Git:

Understand Version Control:

Learn the basics of version control using Git. This is crucial for collaborating on code changes.

Create Feature Branches:

When working on a contribution, create a separate branch for your changes. This keeps the main codebase clean.

7 Writing Quality Code:

Follow Coding Guidelines:

Adhere to the project's coding conventions and guidelines. Consistency is key when collaborating on code.

Write Tests:

If the project has tests, ensure your changes don't break them. If there are no tests, consider adding them as part of your contribution.

8 Submitting a Pull Request:

Follow the Contributing Guide:

Review the project's contributing guide for instructions on submitting pull requests. Provide clear and concise information about your changes.

-Accept Feedback:

Be open to feedback from maintainers and other contributors. Use it as an opportunity to improve your skills.

9 Continuous Contribution:

- Regular Contributions:

Make regular contributions to the project. This demonstrates your commitment and builds a positive relationship with the community.

-Diversify Contributions:

Over time, explore different areas of the project. This could involve working on new features, improving documentation, or assisting with code reviews.

10 Building Your Open Source Profile:

Update Your Portfolio:

Showcase your open-source contributions on platforms like GitHub. This serves as a valuable addition to your coding portfolio.

-Highlight Contributions on Resume:

Mention your open-source contributions on your resume. Employers often value real-world project experience.

11 Giving Back to the Community:

Mentorship:

Once you gain experience, consider mentoring newcomers in the project. Share your knowledge and contribute to the growth of the community.

-Start Your Project:

As you become more confident, think about starting your open-source project. It's a rewarding way to give back to the community.

Contributing to open source is a journey that goes beyond writing code. It's about collaboration, learning, and making a positive impact on the global developer community.

Approach it with enthusiasm, and you'll find it to be a transformative experience in your programming career. Happy coding and contributing!

7

Pair Programming

Pair Programming:

Pair programming is a collaborative coding technique where two programmers work together on the same code. Here's a comprehensive guide on how to effectively engage in pair programming.

1 Understanding Pair Programming:

- Driver and Navigator:

In pair programming, one person takes the role of the "driver" who writes the code, while the other is the "navigator" who reviews each line as it's written.

-Real-Time Collaboration:

It involves real-time collaboration, problem-solving, and continuous communication between the pair.

2 Benefits of Pair Programming:

-Knowledge Sharing:

Pair programming facilitates the exchange of knowledge and skills between team members.

- Fewer Bugs:

With two sets of eyes, there's a higher chance of catching errors and bugs early in the development process.

-Improved Code Quality:

The continuous review process often results in higher code quality and adherence to coding standards.

- Learning Opportunities:

It's an excellent way for less experienced programmers to learn from more experienced ones.

-Enhanced Communication:

Pair programming promotes clear communication, reducing misunderstandings and fostering a shared understanding of the code.

3 Setting Up Pair Programming:

-Choose Roles:

Decide who will be the driver and who will be the navigator. Roles can be switched frequently to maintain balance.

Agree on Goals:

Clearly define the goals of the pair programming session. Whether it's solving a specific problem, implementing a feature, or refactoring code, having a shared objective is crucial.

4 Effective Collaboration:

-Communicate Continuously:

Keep communication lines open throughout the session. Discuss design decisions, code structure, and potential improvements.

-Take Breaks:

Pair programming can be intense. Take short breaks to refresh your mind and maintain focus.

5 Code Reviews in Real Time:

- Immediate Feedback:

Errors and potential issues can be identified and addressed immediately, reducing the need for extensive code reviews later.

-Learning Opportunities:

The navigator can provide insights and suggest improvements, creating valuable learning opportunities for both individuals.

6 Remote Pair Programming:

- Use Collaboration Tools:

Leverage tools like VS Code Live Share, Zoom, or other screen-sharing options for effective remote pair programming.

-Clear Communication:

Ensure clear audio communication and use chat or video features for discussing code.

7 Challenges and Solutions:

-Balancing Contributions:

Ensure both participants have an equal opportunity to contribute. Be mindful of dominating the coding process.

-Handling Disagreements:

Disagreements are normal. Discuss and find compromises to move forward.

8 Learning Resources:

-Pair Programming Exercises:

Practice pair programming with coding exercises to enhance your collaborative coding skills.

- Books and Tutorials:

Explore books like "The Art of Agile Development" by James Shore and "Pair Programming Illuminated" by Laurie Williams for in-depth insights.

9 Implementing in the Workplace:

Introduce Gradually:

If pair programming is new to your team, introduce it gradually. Start with short sessions and gradually increase the duration.

- Collect Feedback:

Regularly collect feedback from team members to assess the effectiveness of pair programming and make necessary adjustments.

10 Reflect and Improve:

-Post-Session Reflection:

After each pair programming session, reflect on what worked well and what could be improved. Use this feedback for continuous improvement.

Pair programming is not just about writing code together; it's about collaboration, communication, and shared learning.

When done effectively, it can significantly enhance the quality of code and the overall development process. Approach pair programming with an open mind, and you'll discover its many benefits in your programming journey. Happy coding!

8

Web Development Fundamentals

Web Development Fundamentals:

Web development is a dynamic field, and understanding its fundamentals is crucial for building effective and scalable web applications. Here's a comprehensive guide to the key concepts and technologies in web development.

Introduction to Web Development:

Client-Side vs. Server-Side:

Web development involves two main components: client-side (front-end) and server-side (back-end). The client-side is what users interact with, while the server-side manages the behind-the-scenes logic and data.

Front-End Development:

HTML (HyperText Markup Language):

-Structure of Web Pages:

HTML is the backbone of web development, defining the structure of web pages through elements like `<html>`, `<head>`, `<body>`, and more.

- Tags and Attributes:

Understand common HTML tags (e.g., `<div>`, `<p>`, `<a>`) and attributes (e.g., `class`, `id`, `src`) to organize and present content.

2.2 CSS (Cascading Style Sheets):

-Styling Web Pages:

CSS is used for styling HTML elements. Learn how to apply styles, colors, fonts, and layouts to create visually appealing websites.

-Selectors and Properties:

Understand CSS selectors (e.g., classes, IDs) and properties (e.g., `color`, `margin`, `padding`) to target and style specific elements.

2.3 JavaScript:

-Dynamic Interactivity:

JavaScript adds interactivity to web pages. Learn how to manipulate the DOM (Document Object Model) and respond to user actions.

-Variables, Functions, and Events:

Master the basics of JavaScript, including declaring variables, defining functions, and handling events triggered by user actions.

2.4 Responsive Design:

- Media Queries:

Implement responsive design using media queries to ensure your web application adapts to different screen sizes and devices.

- Flexbox and Grid:

Utilize Flexbox and CSS Grid for efficient layout design, making it easier to create responsive and flexible interfaces.

3 Back-End Development:

3.1 Server-Side Programming:

-Server-Side Languages:

Choose a server-side language such as Node.js (JavaScript), Python, Ruby, PHP, or Java based on your project requirements.

- Routing and APIs:

Learn how to define routes and create APIs (Application Programming Interfaces) to handle data requests and responses.

3.2 Databases:

-Database Management:

Understand the basics of databases, including SQL (Structured Query Language) for relational databases and NoSQL databases like MongoDB.

-CRUD Operations:

Learn CRUD (Create, Read, Update, Delete) operations to interact with databases and manage data in your web applications.

3.3 Server-Side Frameworks:

-Express (Node.js):

Explore server-side frameworks like Express for Node.js, which simplifies the development of robust and scalable web applications.

-Django (Python), Ruby on Rails (Ruby), Laravel (PHP):

Familiarize yourself with other popular server-side frameworks like Django, Ruby on Rails, and Laravel, each tailored to specific languages.

4 Full-Stack Development:

- Understanding Full-Stack:

Full-stack developers work on both the front-end and back-end of web applications. Develop a proficiency in both areas to become a versatile full-stack developer.

-Communication Between Front-End and Back-End:

Learn how front-end and back-end components communicate through HTTP requests and responses, typically using RESTful APIs.

5 Version Control:

-Git and GitHub:

Master Git for version control, allowing you to track changes, collaborate with others, and manage different versions of your code.

-Branching and Merging:

Understand branching and merging strategies to collaborate effectively with team members and maintain a clean codebase.

6 Deployment:

-Hosting and Deployment Platforms:

Explore hosting platforms like Heroku, Netlify, or Vercel for deploying your web applications. Learn the deployment process for both front-end and back-end.

-Domain Management:

Understand how to manage domain names and configure DNS (Domain Name System) settings for your web applications.

7 Security Best Practices:

-HTTPS:

Implement HTTPS to secure data transmission between clients and servers, preventing unauthorized access.

-Authentication and Authorization:

Learn about authentication (verifying identity) and authorization (granting access) mechanisms to secure your web applications.

8 Web Development Tools:

-Developer Tools:

Familiarize yourself with browser developer tools for debugging, inspecting elements, and optimizing performance.

-Package Managers (npm, yarn):

Use package managers like npm (Node Package Manager) or yarn to manage and install dependencies for your projects.

9 Continuous Learning:

- Stay Updated:

Web development technologies evolve rapidly. Follow blogs, join online communities, and attend conferences to stay informed about the latest trends and best practices.

-Build Real Projects:

Apply your knowledge by working on real projects. This hands-on experience is invaluable for reinforcing concepts and building a strong portfolio.

Web development is a vast and ever-expanding field. As you delve into these fundamentals, remember that practice, curiosity, and continuous learning are essential for mastering the art of web development. Happy coding!

9

Cybersecurity Fundamentals:

Cybersecurity Fundamentals:

Cybersecurity is a critical field focused on protecting computer systems, networks, and data from security breaches, attacks, and unauthorized access.

Here's an extensive guide to understanding the fundamentals of cybersecurity.

1 Introduction to Cybersecurity:

-Definition:

Cybersecurity involves practices, technologies, and processes designed to safeguard computer systems, networks, and data from theft, damage, or unauthorized access.

-Importance:

Cybersecurity is crucial in the digital age to protect sensitive information, maintain privacy, and ensure the integrity of systems.

2 Key Concepts:

2.1 Threats and Attacks:

- Malware:

Malicious software designed to harm or exploit systems, including viruses, worms, Trojans, and ransomware.

-Phishing:

Deceptive attempts to obtain sensitive information, often through fraudulent emails or websites.

-Denial of Service (DoS) Attacks:

Overloading systems with traffic to disrupt normal functioning.

2.2 Cybersecurity Controls:

-Firewalls:

Hardware or software devices that monitor and control incoming and outgoing network traffic.

-Antivirus Software:

Programs designed to detect, prevent, and remove malicious software.

-Encryption:

Converting data into a code to prevent unauthorized access.

2.3 Authentication and Authorization:

-Authentication:

Verifying the identity of users or systems, often through passwords, biometrics, or multi-factor authentication.

-Authorization:

Granting or denying access rights based on authenticated user credentials.

3 Networking Fundamentals:

-Understanding Networks:

Familiarize yourself with networking concepts, including protocols (TCP/IP), routers, switches, and subnets.

-Network Security Protocols:

Learn about secure communication protocols like HTTPS, VPNs, and SSH.

4 Operating System Security:

Secure Configurations:

Implement and maintain secure configurations for operating systems, minimizing vulnerabilities.

-Patch Management:

Regularly update systems with the latest security patches to address known vulnerabilities.

5 Web Security:

-Secure Coding Practices:

Follow secure coding practices to develop resilient web applications.

Web Application Firewalls (WAF):

Deploy WAFs to protect web applications from common vulnerabilities and attacks.

6 Incident Response:

- Incident Detection:

Implement tools and processes to detect security incidents promptly.

-Response Plans:

Develop and regularly update incident response plans to address security breaches effectively.

7 Security Policies and Compliance:

-Security Policies:

Establish and enforce security policies defining acceptable use, access controls, and data handling.

-Compliance Standards:

Adhere to industry-specific and regulatory compliance standards (e.g., GDPR, HIPAA).

8 Security Awareness:

-Training and Education:

Provide ongoing cybersecurity training for employees to raise awareness of potential threats and best practices.

-Social Engineering Awareness:

Educate users about social engineering tactics and how to recognize and avoid them.

9 Penetration Testing and Ethical Hacking:

-Penetration Testing:

Conduct ethical hacking exercises to identify and address vulnerabilities in systems.

-Security Audits:

Regularly audit systems and networks to ensure compliance and identify potential risks.

10 Mobile Security:

-Mobile Device Management (MDM):

Implement MDM solutions to secure and manage mobile devices within an organization.

-App Security:

Emphasize secure coding practices for mobile app development to mitigate security risks.

11Cloud Security:

-Cloud Security Best Practices:

Understand and implement security best practices for cloud-based services and infrastructure.

-Shared Responsibility Model:

Recognize the shared responsibility between cloud service providers and customers for securing data and applications.

12 Threat Intelligence:

-Monitoring Threats:

Stay informed about emerging cybersecurity threats and vulnerabilities.

- Threat Intelligence Platforms:

Use threat intelligence platforms to analyze and respond to evolving threats.

13 Continuous Monitoring:

-Security Information and Event Management (SIEM):

Implement SIEM solutions for continuous monitoring of security events.

- Log Analysis:

Analyze system logs to detect anomalies and potential security incidents.

14 Professional Certifications:

- Certified Information Systems Security Professional (CISSP):

Explore certifications like CISSP, CompTIA Security+, and Certified Ethical Hacker (CEH) to validate cybersecurity expertise.

15 Collaboration and Communication:

-Cross-Functional Collaboration:

Foster collaboration between IT, development, and other departments to ensure a holistic approach to cybersecurity.

-Incident Communication:

Establish clear communication channels for incident reporting and response.

16 Future Trends in Cybersecurity:

-Artificial Intelligence (AI) in Security:

Explore the integration of AI and machine learning for proactive threat detection.

- Zero Trust Architecture:

Embrace the principles of Zero Trust, where no entity is trusted by default, and verification is required from everyone trying to access resources.

Cybersecurity is an ever-evolving field that requires continuous learning and adaptation.

By mastering these fundamentals, you build a strong foundation for navigating the complex landscape of cybersecurity and protecting digital assets effectively. Stay vigilant, stay informed, and stay secure.

10

Artificial Intelligence and Machine Learning Fundamentals

Artificial Intelligence and Machine Learning Fundamentals:

Artificial Intelligence (AI) and Machine Learning (ML) are transformative technologies that enable computers to perform tasks traditionally requiring human intelligence.

Here's an extensive guide to understanding the fundamentals of AI and ML.

1 Introduction to Artificial Intelligence:

-Definition:

AI refers to the development of computer systems that can perform tasks that typically require human intelligence, such as visual perception, speech recognition, decision-making, and language translation.

-Types of AI:

AI can be categorized into Narrow or Weak AI, which is designed for a specific task, and General or Strong AI, which exhibits intelligence across a wide range of tasks.

2 Machine Learning Basics:

-Definition:

ML is a subset of AI that focuses on developing algorithms and models that allow computers to learn from data and make predictions or decisions without explicit programming.

-Supervised Learning:

In supervised learning, models are trained on labeled data, where the input-output pairs are provided for learning. Common tasks include classification and regression.

-Unsupervised Learning:

Unsupervised learning involves training models on unlabeled data to identify patterns or groupings within the data. Clustering and dimensionality reduction are common unsupervised tasks.

-Reinforcement Learning:

Reinforcement learning involves training agents to make sequences of decisions in an environment to maximize a cumulative reward. It's often used in game playing and robotics.

3 Key Machine Learning Concepts:

3.1 Features and Labels:

-Features:

Features are the input variables used to make predictions or decisions in a machine learning model.

-Labels:

Labels are the outputs or predictions generated by the model.

3.2 Training and Testing Data:

-Training Data:

Training data is used to train the model by adjusting its parameters to minimize the difference between predicted and actual outcomes.

Testing Data:

Testing data is used to evaluate the model's performance on new, unseen data.

3.3 Model Evaluation Metrics:

- Accuracy:

Accuracy measures the percentage of correctly predicted instances in classification tasks.

- Mean Squared Error (MSE):

MSE is commonly used in regression tasks to measure the average squared difference between predicted and actual values.

3.4 Overfitting and Underfitting:

- Overfitting:

Overfitting occurs when a model performs well on training data but poorly on new data. It indicates that the model has learned noise in the training data.

-Underfitting:

Underfitting occurs when a model is too simple to capture the underlying patterns in the data, resulting in poor performance on both training and new data.

4 Popular Machine Learning Algorithms:

4.1 Supervised Learning Algorithms:

-Linear Regression:

Used for predicting a continuous outcome based on one or more input features.

-Decision Trees:

Tree-like models that make decisions based on the values of input features.

-Support Vector Machines (SVM):

Used for classification tasks by finding the optimal hyperplane that separates different classes.

-Neural Networks:

Deep learning models composed of layers of interconnected nodes, inspired by the structure of the human brain.

4.2 Unsupervised Learning Algorithms:

-K-Means Clustering:

Divides data into k clusters based on similarity.

- Principal Component Analysis (PCA):

Reduces the dimensionality of data while preserving its variance.

-Association Rule Learning:

Identifies patterns or associations in data, commonly used in market basket analysis.

5 Deep Learning:

-Neural Networks:

Deep learning models are composed of neural networks with multiple layers (deep neural networks).

- Convolutional Neural Networks (CNN):

Specialized for image recognition tasks, CNNs use convolutional layers to extract features.

- Recurrent Neural Networks (RNN):

Suitable for sequence-based tasks, RNNs have connections that form directed cycles.

6 Natural Language Processing (NLP):

-Definition:

NLP involves the interaction between computers and human language, enabling machines to understand, interpret, and generate human-like text.

-Applications:

NLP is used in sentiment analysis, chatbots, language translation, and information retrieval.

7 Reinforcement Learning:

-Agents and Environments:

In reinforcement learning, an agent interacts with an environment, making decisions to maximize a cumulative reward.

-Q-Learning and Deep Q Networks (DQN):

Algorithms used in reinforcement learning for decision-making in dynamic environments.

8 Model Deployment:

- Scalability:

Consider scalability when deploying models to ensure they can handle varying workloads.

-APIs and Microservices:

Deploy models as APIs or microservices for seamless integration with other applications.

9. Ethics in AI:

- Bias and Fairness:

Address biases in data and models to ensure fairness and prevent discriminatory outcomes.

- Transparency and Accountability:

Promote transparency in AI decision-making and hold developers and organizations accountable for the ethical use of AI.

10 Continuous Learning:

-Stay Updated:

AI and ML are rapidly evolving fields; stay informed about new algorithms, techniques, and research.

-Hands-On Projects:

Apply your knowledge through hands-on projects to reinforce concepts and build a strong portfolio.

Artificial Intelligence and Machine Learning are powerful tools with the potential to revolutionize various industries.

By mastering these fundamentals, you'll be well-equipped to contribute to the advancement of AI and ML applications. Keep exploring, experimenting, and contributing to the exciting world of intelligent systems.

11

Version Control Mastery: Navigating Code Evolution with Git

Version Control Mastery: Navigating Code Evolution with Git

1. Understanding Version Control:

- Definition:

Version control is a system that records changes to files over time, enabling you to recall specific versions later.

- Importance:

Facilitates collaboration, tracks project history, and provides a safety net for code changes.

2. Introduction to Git:

- What is Git:

Git is a distributed version control system that allows multiple contributors to work on a project simultaneously.

-Key Concepts:

Understand terms like repositories, commits, branches, and merges.

3. Setting Up Git:

- Installation:

Install Git on your local machine by following the platform-specific instructions.

-Configuration:

Configure Git with your name, email, and preferred settings using the command line.

4. Basic Git Commands:

- git init:
    - Initialize a new Git repository.

- git add:

Stage changes for the next commit.

- git commit:

Record changes to the repository.

5. Branching Strategies:

-Creating Branches:

Use branches to isolate work on new features or fixes.

- Merging Branches:

Merge branches back into the main codebase using Git merge.

6. Remote Repositories:

- Cloning:

Clone repositories from remote sources to your local machine.

-Push and Pull:

Push changes to a remote repository or pull changes from it.

7. Collaboration with Git:

-Forking:

Fork a repository to contribute to someone else's project.

-Pull Requests:

Propose changes to the main project through pull requests.

8. Resolving Conflicts:

-Conflict Identification:

Learn to identify and understand merge conflicts.

-Manual Resolution:

Resolve conflicts manually by editing code files.

9. Git Tags:

- Creating Tags:

Tag specific points in Git history for easy reference.

-Annotated vs. Lightweight Tags:

Understand the difference between annotated and lightweight tags.

10. Git Workflow Strategies:

-Feature Branch Workflow:

Develop new features in dedicated branches.

- Gitflow Workflow:

Adopt the Gitflow model for more complex project structures.

11. Git Best Practices:

Commit Messages:

Write clear and concise commit messages.

-Frequent Commits:

Make smaller, more frequent commits for easier tracking.

12. Git GUI Tools:

- SourceTree, GitKraken, etc.:

Explore Git GUI tools to visualize branches and changes.

-Integrations with IDEs:

Integrate Git with your preferred Integrated Development Environment (IDE).

13. Git and Continuous Integration:

-Integration with CI/CD Tools:

Incorporate Git into Continuous Integration/Continuous Deployment (CI/CD) pipelines.

-Automated Testing:

Implement automated testing to catch issues early in development.

14. Git Security Practices:

-SSH Keys:

Use SSH keys for secure authentication with remote repositories.

-Access Control:

Implement access controls to restrict repository access.

15. Git in Real-World Projects:

- Open Source Contributions:

Explore contributing to open-source projects using Git.

-Enterprise Use:

Understand how Git scales for enterprise-level projects.

16. Troubleshooting in Git:

-Reverting Commits:

Learn how to revert commits in case of mistakes.

-Git Reflog:

Use Git reflog to recover lost commits.

17. Git Etiquette:

Branch Naming Conventions:

Adopt consistent branch-naming conventions.

- Code Reviews:

Participate in and conduct effective code reviews.

18. Git Documentation and Resources:

-Official Git Documentation:

Refer to the official Git documentation for in-depth information.

-Online Courses and Tutorials:

Explore online courses and tutorials to enhance your Git skills.

19. Git and DevOps:

-Versioning in DevOps:

Integrate Git versioning into DevOps practices.

-Infrastructure as Code:

Manage infrastructure changes with Git through Infrastructure as Code (IaC).

20. Continuous Learning and Community Engagement:

-Git Community:

Engage with the Git community for updates and support.

-Contribute to Git Projects:

Consider contributing to Git-related projects to deepen your understanding.

Mastering Git opens the door to efficient collaboration, streamlined development workflows, and effective version control.

By following best practices, exploring advanced features, and actively participating in the Git community, you'll not only become proficient but contribute to the collaborative spirit that makes Git an invaluable tool in the world of   software   development.

12

Embracing Networking

Embracing Networking: Unlocking Opportunities through Meetups and Conferences

1. Understanding the Value of Networking:

-Professional Growth:

Networking at meetups and conferences is essential for expanding your professional circle and fostering growth.

-Learning Opportunities:

Gain insights into the latest industry trends, technologies, and best practices.

2. Locating Local Meetups:

- Online Platforms:

Explore platforms like Meetup.com, Eventbrite, or local tech community websites.

-Tech Hubs:

Check out local tech hubs, co-working spaces, or university campuses for recurring meetups.

3. Choosing Relevant Conferences:

- Research:

Explore conferences related to your field through online research and recommendations.

-Industry Events:

Attend conferences organized by renowned industry associations for comprehensive insights.

4.Preparing for Events:

-Review Agenda:

Familiarize yourself with the event agenda to plan which sessions to attend.

Bring Business Cards:

Have business cards ready for seamless networking.

5. Active Participation:

-Engage in Discussions:

Participate actively in discussions during meetups and Q&A sessions at conferences.

- Networking Breaks:

Utilize breaks for networking opportunities and connecting with fellow attendees.

6. Building Your Elevator Pitch:

-Introduction:

Craft a concise elevator pitch introducing yourself, your skills, and your interests.

-Expressing Goals:

Clearly articulate your professional goals during networking interactions.

7. Joining Tech Communities:

- Online Platforms:

Join tech communities on platforms like GitHub, Stack Overflow, or specialized forums.

- Local Tech Groups:

Participate in local tech groups on social media or community websites.

8..Benefits of Networking:

-Job Opportunities:

Discover job opportunities and career advancement possibilities.

-Knowledge Sharing:

Exchange knowledge with peers and stay informed about industry developments.

9. Effective Networking Strategies:

-Active Listening:

Practice active listening to understand others' perspectives and experiences.

-Reciprocity:

Offer help and insights to others, fostering a culture of reciprocity.

10. Overcoming Networking Challenges:

- Introverted Professionals:

Develop strategies for networking if you identify as introverted.

- Navigating Crowds:

Techniques for navigating crowded events and approaching new connections.

11. Conference Attendance Etiquette:

- Respecting Presenters:

Respect presenters by arriving on time and refraining from distracting behaviors.

- Question Etiquette:

Pose thoughtful questions during Q&A sessions, contributing positively.

12. Post-Event Follow-Up:

-Connect on Professional Platforms:

Connect with new acquaintances on professional platforms like LinkedIn.

Express Gratitude:

Express gratitude to speakers or organizers via email or social media.

13.Creating Your Personal Brand:

-Consistent Online Presence:

Maintain a consistent and professional online presence through platforms like LinkedIn or a personal website.

-Contributing to Discussions:

Contribute to online discussions to showcase your expertise.

14. Staying Informed:

- Industry News:

Keep yourself informed about the latest industry news and trends.

- Continuous Learning:

Attend meetups or webinars focused on continuous learning.

15. International Conferences and Diversity:

-Global Perspectives:

Consider attending international conferences for diverse perspectives.

- Inclusivity:

Promote inclusivity and diversity within the tech community.

16. Creating Your Meetup or Conference Presence:

- Lightning Talks:

Consider presenting a lightning talk to showcase your expertise.

-Organizing Workshops:

Host workshops to share your knowledge with others.

17. Balancing Networking and Learning:

-Strategic Breaks:

Find a balance between networking and attending sessions for optimal learning.

- Setting Goals:

Set specific networking goals for each event.

18. Measuring Networking Success:

- Quality Connections:

Measure success by the quality of connections made, not just quantity.

- Collaborative Opportunities:

Gauge success through collaborative opportunities that arise from networking.

19. Creating a Long-Term Network:

- Follow-Up Periodically:

Periodically check in with connections to nurture long-term relationships.

- Contributing to the Community:

Contribute to the community by sharing your experiences and insights.

20. Adapting to Virtual Networking:

- Online Platforms:

Leverage virtual platforms for networking in the absence of physical events.

- Participate in Virtual Meetups:

Actively participate in virtual meetups and conferences.

Networking at meetups and conferences is a powerful strategy for career advancement and staying abreast of industry trends.

By adopting effective networking strategies, maintaining a positive online presence, and actively participating in the tech community, you can build a strong professional network that opens doors to new opportunities and enriches your career   journey.

13

Mastering Algorithms and Data Structures

Mastering Algorithms and Data Structures: The Foundation of Efficient Programming

1. Introduction to Algorithms and Data Structures:

- Definition:

Algorithms are step-by-step procedures or formulas for solving problems, while data structures are the way data is organized and stored in a computer.

- Importance:

Fundamentals for writing efficient and scalable code.

2. The Role of Algorithms:

- Problem Solving:

Algorithms provide systematic approaches to problem-solving.

- Efficiency:

Well-designed algorithms optimize the use of computational resources.

3. Types of Algorithms:

- Searching Algorithms:

Sequential search, binary search, and more.

- Sorting Algorithms:

Bubble sort, quicksort, mergesort, and others.

4. Understanding Data Structures:

- Arrays:

Simple, yet powerful for storing data.

-Linked Lists:

Dynamic structures facilitating easy insertion and deletion.

- Stacks and Queues:

LIFO (Last In, First Out) and FIFO (First In, First Out) structures.

5. Trees:

- Binary Trees:

Hierarchical structures with at most two children.

- Balanced Trees:

AVL trees, Red-Black trees for efficient searching.

6. Graphs:

- Representation:

Adjacency matrices, adjacency lists for graph storage.

- Traversal:

Depth-First Search (DFS) and Breadth-First Search (BFS).

7. Hashing:

- Hash Functions:

Converting data into fixed-size values for efficient retrieval.

- Collision Resolution:

Handling cases when two items hash to the same location.

8. Dynamic Programming:

- Optimization Technique:

Breaking down problems into smaller subproblems to avoid redundant computations.

-Memoization:

Caching results to optimize recursive algorithms.

9. Greedy Algorithms:

- Optimal Solutions:

Making locally optimal choices to achieve a global optimum.

- Applications:

Huffman coding, Dijkstra's algorithm.

10. Complexity Analysis:

- Time Complexity:

Evaluating how the running time of an algorithm increases with the size of the input.

- Space Complexity:

Analyzing the memory usage of an algorithm.

11. Big-O Notation:

-Asymptotic Analysis:

Describing the upper bound of an algorithm's running time.

- Common Classes:

$O(1)$, $O(\log n)$, $O(n)$, $O(n \log n)$, $O(n^2)$, etc.

12. Practical Implementation:

- Choosing the Right Algorithm:

Selecting algorithms based on the problem requirements.

-Code Optimization:

Writing code with efficiency in mind.

13. Algorithm Design Paradigms:

- Divide and Conquer:

Breaking down problems into simpler subproblems.

- Backtracking:

Trying out different possibilities and reverting when necessary.

14. Tree and Graph Algorithms:

- Traversal Techniques:

Preorder, inorder, postorder traversals for trees.

- Shortest Path Algorithms:

Dijkstra's algorithm, Bellman-Ford algorithm.

15. Sorting Algorithms in Depth:

- Quicksort:

Efficient divide-and-conquer sorting algorithm.

- Mergesort:

Divide, conquer, and merge approach.

16. Algorithm Challenges:

-Online Platforms:

Participating in coding challenges on platforms like LeetCode and HackerRank.

- Competitive Programming:

Engaging in competitive programming for real-world problem-solving.

17. Resources for Learning:

- Books:

"Introduction to Algorithms" by Cormen et al.

-Online Courses:

Platforms like Coursera, edX, and Khan Academy offer courses on algorithms and data structures.

18. Continuous Learning:

-Stay Updated:

Regularly explore new algorithms and data structures.

- Community Engagement:

Join coding communities to discuss and learn from others.

19. Application in Real-World Projects:

-Optimizing Code:

Apply learned algorithms to optimize code in real-world projects.

- Handling Large Datasets:

Efficiently process and manipulate large datasets.

20. Teaching and Mentoring:

- Knowledge Sharing:

Contribute to the learning community by sharing your knowledge.

-Mentoring:

Mentor others to reinforce your understanding and help them grow.

Conclusion:

Mastering algorithms and data structures is a journey that transforms your problem-solving skills and lays the groundwork for becoming a proficient programmer.

By understanding the principles, practicing through coding challenges, and staying engaged with the coding community, you'll not only enhance your programming abilities but also contribute to the evolving landscape of efficient software   development.

14

Embarking on Mobile App Development

Embarking on Mobile App Development: Unleashing Creativity with Android (Java/Kotlin) and iOS (Swift)

1. Introduction to Mobile App Development:

- Definition:

Mobile app development involves creating software applications specifically for mobile devices.

- Platforms:

Primary platforms include Android (Java/Kotlin) and iOS (Swift).

2. Understanding Android Development:

- Android Studio:

Android's official integrated development environment (IDE).

- Java vs. Kotlin:

Choose between Java and Kotlin for Android development.

3. Setting Up Android Development Environment:

-Installation:

Download and set up Android Studio on your machine.

-SDK and Emulators:

Install the required Software Development Kit (SDK) and emulators for testing.

4. Android App Components:

- Activities:

Represent screens in Android apps.

- Fragments:

Reusable portions of UI within an activity.

5. User Interface Design in Android:

- XML Layouts:

Design app layouts using XML.

- UI Components:

Buttons, text fields, and more for interactive interfaces.

6. Event Handling and User Input:

- Listeners:

Handle user interactions through event listeners.

- Input Validation:

Ensure data entered by users is valid.

7. Data Storage in Android:

-Shared Preferences:

Store key-value pairs for lightweight data.

SQLite Database:

Implement a local database for more complex data structures.

8.Networking in Android:

- HTTP Requests:

Communicate with web servers through HTTP requests.

-Asynchronous Processing:

Use AsyncTask or other methods for non-blocking operations.

9. Integrating Third-Party Libraries:

- Retrofit for Networking:

Integrate Retrofit for efficient HTTP requests.

-Glide for Image Loading:

Use Glide for seamless image loading.

10. Testing and Debugging in Android:

- Unit Testing:

Write and execute unit tests for code components.

- Debugging Tools:

Utilize Android Studio's debugging tools.

11. Deploying Android Apps:

- Generating APKs:

Create APKs for distribution.

- Google Play Store:

Publish apps on the Google Play Store.

12. Introduction to iOS Development:

- Xcode:

Apple's official IDE for iOS development.

- Swift Programming Language:

Primary language for iOS development.

13. Setting Up iOS Development Environment:

- Xcode Installation:

Download and set up Xcode on your macOS machine.

- iOS Simulators:

Explore and use iOS simulators for testing.

14. iOS App Components:

- ViewControllers:

Manage user interfaces and user interactions.

- Storyboard:

Visual representation of the app's flow.

15. User Interface Design in iOS:

- Interface Builder:

Design app interfaces using Interface Builder.

- Auto Layout:

Ensure responsive design across different iOS devices.

16. Event Handling and User Input in iOS:

- Actions and Outlets:

Connect UI elements to code through actions and outlets.

- Gesture Recognizers:

Handle gestures for enhanced user interactions.

17. Data Storage in iOS:

- UserDefaults:

Store user preferences and simple data.

- Core Data:

Implement a robust data storage solution.

18. Networking in iOS:

- NSURLSession:

Communicate with web servers using NSURLSession.

- Asynchronous Programming:

Use closures for asynchronous operations.

19. Integrating Third-Party Libraries in iOS:

- CocoaPods:

Manage dependencies using CocoaPods.

- Alamofire for Networking:

Integrate Alamofire for simplified networking.

20. Testing and Debugging in iOS:

- XCTest:

Write unit tests with XCTest.

- Debugging in Xcode:

Utilize Xcode's debugging features.

21. Deploying iOS Apps:

-Generating IPA Files:

Create IPA files for distribution.

-App Store Connect:

Submit apps for review and distribution on the App Store.

22. Cross-Platform Development:

- Flutter and React Native:

Explore cross-platform frameworks for simultaneous Android and iOS development.

- Pros and Cons:

Weigh the advantages and disadvantages of cross-platform development.

23. Continuous Learning and Updates:

- Stay Informed:

Regularly check for updates in Android and iOS development tools.

-Community Involvement:

Engage with the developer communities for ongoing learning.

Conclusion:

Mobile app development offers a canvas for innovation and creativity. By mastering Android and iOS development, understanding the intricacies of each platform, and staying abreast of industry trends, you'll not only build functional and visually appealing apps but also contribute to the dynamic and ever-evolving world of mobile technology.

15

Unlocking the Power of Database Management Systems

Unlocking the Power of Database Management Systems: A Comprehensive Guide

1.Introduction to Database Management Systems (DBMS):

- Definition:

DBMS is software designed to manage, store, and retrieve data efficiently.

-Importance:

Crucial for organizing, accessing, and manipulating data in various applications.

2. Types of Database Management Systems:

- Relational Database Management Systems (RDBMS):

Structured data with predefined relationships (e.g., MySQL, PostgreSQL).

- NoSQL Database Management Systems:

Dynamic and unstructured data (e.g., MongoDB, Cassandra).

3. Setting Up a Relational Database (MySQL):

- Installation:

Download and install MySQL on your server or local machine.

-Configuration:

Configure user accounts, security settings, and other parameters.

4. Basic SQL Commands:

- SELECT Statement:

Retrieve data from one or more tables.

- INSERT Statement:

Add new data into tables.

- UPDATE Statement:

Modify existing data.

-DELETE Statement:

Remove data from tables.

5. Database Design Principles:

- Normalization:

Organize data to minimize redundancy and improve efficiency.

- Indexes:

Enhance query performance by creating indexes on columns.

6. Transactions and ACID Properties:

- Atomicity:

Ensures that transactions are treated as a single, indivisible unit.

-Consistency:

Maintains data integrity and enforces predefined rules.

- Isolation:

Ensures that one transaction doesn't interfere with another.

-Durability:

Guarantees that committed transactions are permanent.

7. Relational Database Modeling:

-Entity-Relationship Diagrams (ERD):

Visual representation of database entities and their relationships.

- Primary and Foreign Keys:

Define relationships between tables using keys.

8. Advanced SQL Concepts:

- Joins:

Combine data from multiple tables.

- Subqueries:

Nest queries within other queries.

9. Introduction to NoSQL Databases (MongoDB):

- Document-Oriented Structure:

Store data in flexible, JSON-like documents.

-Collections:

Equivalent to tables in relational databases.

10. Setting Up MongoDB:

- Installation:

Download and install MongoDB on your system.

- Configuration:

Configure MongoDB settings, users, and security.

11. Basic MongoDB Operations:

- Inserting Documents:

Add documents to collections.

- Querying Data:

Retrieve data using MongoDB queries.

- Updating and Deleting Documents:

Modify or remove existing documents.

12. NoSQL Data Modeling:

-Denormalization:

Store redundant data for improved query performance.

-Embedding vs. Referencing:

Choose between embedding documents or referencing other collections.

13. Indexing in MongoDB:

- Creating Indexes:

Improve query performance by creating indexes.

-Types of Indexes:

Single field, compound, text indexes, and more.

14. Database Security:

- Authentication and Authorization:

Implement user authentication and assign appropriate privileges.

- Encryption:

Secure data transmission and storage using encryption.

15. Backup and Recovery:

-Regular Backups:

Establish a routine backup strategy.

- Point-in-Time Recovery:

Recover databases to a specific point in time.

16. Database Scaling Strategies:

- Vertical Scaling:

Increase server capacity (CPU, RAM).

-Horizontal Scaling:

Distribute data across multiple servers.

17. Data Migration and ETL:

- ETL Process:

Extract, Transform, Load data between databases.

- Tools and Best Practices:

Explore tools and best practices for seamless data migration.

18. Database Performance Optimization:

-Query Optimization:

Analyze and optimize query execution plans.

-Monitoring Tools:

Use monitoring tools to identify performance bottlenecks.

19. Database as a Service (DBaaS):

- Cloud Database Solutions:

Utilize cloud-based database services for scalability and flexibility.

- Advantages and Considerations:

Understand the pros and cons of DBaaS.

20. Continual Learning and Community Engagement:

-Online Courses and Certifications:

Enroll in courses to deepen your knowledge.

- Engage in Forums:

Participate in online forums and communities for discussions and problem-solving.

Conclusion:

Database management is the backbone of data-driven applications. By mastering both relational and NoSQL database systems, understanding key concepts, and embracing best practices, you'll not only become proficient in designing efficient databases but also contribute to the seamless functioning of applications that rely on organized and accessible data.

16

Embarking on the Journey of Machine Learning and Artificial Intelligence

Embarking on the Journey of Machine Learning and Artificial Intelligence: Unleashing the Power of Data Analysis and Predictive Modeling

1. Introduction to Machine Learning (ML) and Artificial Intelligence (AI):

-Definition:

ML is a subset of AI that enables systems to learn from data and make predictions.

- Importance:

Revolutionizes data analysis, decision-making, and automation.

2.Types of Machine Learning:

-Supervised Learning:

Learn from labeled data with input-output pairs.

-Unsupervised Learning'

Extract patterns from unlabeled data.

- Reinforcement Learning:

Learn through interaction with an environment and rewards.

3. Setting Up a Machine Learning Environment:

-Python and Jupyter Notebooks:

Use Python as the primary language and Jupyter Notebooks for interactive development.

- Libraries:

Essential libraries include NumPy, Pandas, Matplotlib, and Scikit-Learn.

4. Exploratory Data Analysis (EDA):

- Data Visualization:

Use Matplotlib and Seaborn for visualizing data distributions.

-Descriptive Statistics:

Analyze key statistics to understand data characteristics.

5. Data Preprocessing:

- Handling Missing Data:

Impute or remove missing values.

-Feature Scaling:

Normalize or standardize features for uniformity.

6. Supervised Learning Algorithms:

- Linear Regression:

Predict a continuous variable based on linear relationships.

-Logistic Regression:

Classify data into discrete categories.

- Decision Trees and Random Forest:

Construct tree-like models for classification and regression.

7. Model Evaluation and Hyperparameter Tuning:

- Train-Test Split:

Split data into training and testing sets for evaluation.

-Cross-Validation:

Assess model performance using k-fold cross-validation.

8. Unsupervised Learning Algorithms:

- K-Means Clustering:

Group data points based on similarity.

- Principal Component Analysis (PCA):

Reduce dimensionality for complex datasets.

9. Natural Language Processing (NLP):

-Text Preprocessing:

Tokenization, stemming, and lemmatization.

- Sentiment Analysis:

Determine sentiments from textual data.

10. Reinforcement Learning Concepts:

- Markov Decision Processes (MDP):

Formulate problems for reinforcement learning.

- Q-Learning:

Implement Q-learning for decision-making.

11. Deep Learning and Neural Networks:

- Artificial Neural Networks (ANN):

Understand the basics of neural networks.

- Deep Learning Frameworks:

TensorFlow and PyTorch for building complex models.

12. Convolutional Neural Networks (CNN):

- Image Classification:

Implement CNNs for image recognition tasks.

- Transfer Learning:

Leverage pre-trained models for specific tasks.

13. Recurrent Neural Networks (RNN):

- Sequential Data Analysis:

Process sequences for tasks like language modeling.

- Long Short-Term Memory (LSTM):

Address vanishing gradient problem in RNNs.

14. Evaluation Metrics for ML Models:

- Accuracy, Precision, Recall:

Assess classification models.

-Mean Squared Error (MSE), R-squared:

Evaluate regression models.

15. Deployment and Productionizing Models:

- Model Serialization:

Save models for future use.

-APIs and Web Services:

Deploy models as APIs for integration.

16. Model Interpretability and Explainability:

- Feature Importance:

Identify key features contributing to model predictions.

-LIME and SHAP:

Tools for interpreting complex models.

17. Ethical Considerations in AI:

- Bias and Fairness:

Address biases in training data and models.

- Transparency:

Strive for transparent AI systems.

18. Continuous Learning and Staying Updated:

-Research Papers and Journals:

Follow leading research in ML and AI.

-Online Courses and Conferences:

Enroll in courses and attend conferences for continuous learning.

19. Real-World Applications of ML and AI:

-Healthcare:

Diagnosis, personalized medicine.

- Finance:

Fraud detection, risk assessment.

-E-commerce:

Recommendation systems, customer segmentation.

20.Contributing to AI Community and Open Source:

-GitHub Contributions:

Share code, projects, and collaborate with the community.

- Mentoring:

Mentor aspiring AI enthusiasts to foster knowledge exchange.

Conclusion:

Machine Learning and Artificial Intelligence empower data-driven decision-making and predictive modeling.

By mastering foundational concepts, staying abreast of evolving techniques, and contributing to the vibrant AI community, you'll not only advance your career but also contribute to the transformative impact of AI on various industries.

17

Embarking on the Adventure of Game Development

Embarking on the Adventure of Game Development: Unleashing Creativity with Unity and Unreal Engine

Introduction to Game Development:

- Definition:

Game development is the process of creating interactive experiences for players.

-Importance:

Merges creativity, programming, and design for immersive experiences.

2. Choosing a Game Development Engine:

-Unity:

Versatile and widely used for 2D and 3D games.

-Unreal Engine:

Known for high-end graphics and popular for AAA titles.

3. Setting Up the Development Environment:

-Unity Hub:

Manage Unity projects and versions.

-Epic Games Launcher:

Access Unreal Engine and project management tools.

4.Understanding Game Objects and Assets:

- Unity Prefabs:

Reusable and modular game objects.

-Unreal Engine Actors:

Fundamental units in the game world.

5.Scripting in Unity (C#) and Unreal Engine (Blueprints):

- Unity Scripting:

Use C# for logic and behavior.

- Unreal Engine Blueprints:

Visual scripting for game logic.

6. Physics and Collision:

- Unity Physics Engine:

Implement realistic movement and collision.

-Unreal Engine Physics:

Utilize the built-in physics system.

7.Animation and Rigging:

- Unity Animator:

Create animations and control transitions.

-Unreal Engine Animation System:

Rig characters and animate using Sequencer.

8. User Interface (UI) Design:

- Unity UI Elements:

Design interactive menus and HUDs.

-Unreal Engine UMG (Unreal Motion Graphics):

Create UI elements using visual scripting.

9. Game Mechanics and Logic:

- Unity State Machines:

Implement game logic using state machines.

- Unreal Engine Gameplay Framework:

Develop game mechanics using Blueprints.

10. Audio Integration:

-Unity Audio System:

Integrate sound effects and music.

- Unreal Engine Audio Mixer:

Control and mix audio elements.

11. Optimizing Game Performance:

-Unity Profiler:

Analyze and optimize game performance.

-Unreal Engine Performance Tools:

Use built-in tools for profiling.

12. Creating 3D Environments:

-Unity Terrain System:

Design landscapes and terrain.

-Unreal Engine Landscape:

Sculpt and paint vast landscapes.

13. Lighting and Shading:

- Unity Lighting:

Implement dynamic lighting and shadows.

-Unreal Engine Lighting System:

Utilize realistic global illumination.

14. Particle Systems and Special Effects:

-Unity Particle System:

Create dynamic visual effects.

- Unreal Engine Cascade:

Design particle effects.

15. Building and Deploying Games:

- Unity Build Settings:

Configure build settings for various platforms.

- Unreal Engine Packaging:

Package games for distribution.

16. Augmented Reality (AR) and Virtual Reality (VR):

-Unity AR Foundation:

Develop AR experiences.

- Unreal Engine VR Development:

Create immersive VR environments.

17. Multiplayer and Networking:

-Unity Multiplayer Services:

Implement online multiplayer features.

- Unreal Engine Networking:

Create multiplayer games with Blueprint.

18. Game Testing and Debugging:

-Unity Play Mode:

Test games within the Unity editor.

-Unreal Engine Playtesting:

Debug and test game functionality.

19. Continuous Learning and Community Engagement:

-Online Courses and Tutorials:

Enroll in game development courses.

-Game Development Forums:

Engage with game development communities.

20. Publishing and Marketing Your Game:

-Steam, App Store, Google Play:

Publish games on popular platforms.

-Social Media and Marketing:

Build a community and market your game.

Conclusion:

Game development is a dynamic and rewarding field that blends technical skills with artistic creativity.

By mastering Unity or Unreal Engine, understanding key concepts, and actively participating in the game development community, you'll not only bring your game ideas to life but also contribute to the vibrant world of interactive entertainment.

18

Mastering Cloud Computing

Mastering Cloud Computing: Navigating AWS, Azure, and Google Cloud for Scalable Solutions

1. Introduction to Cloud Computing:

- Definition:

Cloud computing provides on-demand access to a shared pool of computing resources over the internet.

- Benefits:

Scalability, flexibility, cost-efficiency.

2. Major Cloud Service Providers:

- Amazon Web Services (AWS):

Offers a wide range of cloud services and products.

- Microsoft Azure:

Microsoft's cloud platform with diverse services.

- Google Cloud Platform (GCP):

Google's suite of cloud services and infrastructure.

3. Getting Started:

- Creating Accounts:

Sign up for AWS, Azure, or GCP accounts.

- Dashboard and Console Navigation:

Explore the dashboard and navigation within each platform.

4. Compute Services:

-AWS EC2 (Elastic Compute Cloud):

Launch and manage virtual servers.

-Azure Virtual Machines:

Deploy and scale virtual machines.

-GCP Compute Engine:

Create and manage virtual machines.

5. Storage Solutions:

- AWS S3 (Simple Storage Service):

Store and retrieve any amount of data.

-Azure Blob Storage:

Object storage for unstructured data.

-GCP Cloud Storage:

Store and access data globally.

6. Database Services:

-AWS RDS (Relational Database Service):

Managed relational database service.

-Azure SQL Database:

Fully managed relational database.

-GCP Cloud SQL:

Managed relational databases in the cloud.

7. Networking in the Cloud:

-Virtual Networks:

Set up and configure virtual networks.

-Load Balancing:

Distribute incoming network traffic.

8. Serverless Computing:

- AWS Lambda:

Run code without provisioning or managing servers.

-Azure Functions:

Execute code in response to events.

-GCP Cloud Functions:

Execute functions in response to events.

9. Containers and Orchestration:

-AWS ECS (Elastic Container Service):

Run and scale containerized applications.

- Azure Kubernetes Service (AKS):

Simplify deployment, management, and operations of Kubernetes.

- GCP Kubernetes Engine:

Host and manage Kubernetes clusters.

10. Identity and Access Management (IAM):

- AWS IAM:

Manage access to AWS resources securely.

- Azure Active Directory:

Identity and access management service.

- GCP Identity and Access Management:

Control access to resources in GCP.

11. Security in the Cloud:

-AWS Security Groups:

Virtual firewalls controlling inbound/outbound traffic.

- Azure Security Center:

Monitor and strengthen security posture.

- GCP Security Command Center:

Gain insights into security risks.

12. Monitoring and Logging:

- AWS CloudWatch:

Monitor AWS resources and applications.

- Azure Monitor:

Collect and analyze telemetry data.

- GCP Stackdriver:

Monitor, log, and diagnose.

13. Cost Management:

-AWS Cost Explorer:

Analyze and visualize AWS costs.

-Azure Cost Management:

Optimize and manage Azure costs.

-GCP Cost Management Tools:

Monitor and control GCP costs.

14. Hybrid and Multi-Cloud Solutions:

-AWS Outposts:

Extend AWS infrastructure on-premises.

-Azure Hybrid Cloud:

Combine on-premises and cloud services.

-GCP Anthos:

Hybrid and multi-cloud platform.

15. Certifications and Training:

-AWS Certifications:

Solutions Architect, Developer, SysOps Administrator, etc.

-Azure Certifications:

AZ-900, AZ-104, AZ-204, etc.

-GCP Certifications:

Associate Cloud Engineer, Professional Cloud Architect, etc.

16. Real-World Use Cases:

- Startups:

Cost-effective infrastructure for new ventures.

- Enterprise Solutions:

Scalable and secure solutions for established businesses.

- Big Data and Analytics:

Process and analyze vast datasets in the cloud.

17. Continuous Learning and Community Engagement:

- Official Documentation:

Explore comprehensive documentation provided by each cloud provider.

- Community Forums and Events:

Engage with the cloud computing community for knowledge exchange.

18. Case Studies and Best Practices:

-AWS Success Stories:

Learn from businesses thriving on AWS.

- Azure Customer Stories:

Explore how companies leverage Azure.

-GCP Case Studies:

Understand successful GCP implementations.

19. Ethical Considerations in Cloud Computing:

-Data Privacy and Compliance:

Adhere to privacy regulations and compliance standards.

- Security Protocols:

Implement robust security measures.

20. Contributing to Cloud Community and Open Source:

- GitHub Contributions:

Share scripts, templates, and contribute to open-source projects.

- Mentoring:

Mentor others entering the cloud computing domain.

Conclusion:

Mastering cloud computing is pivotal in the era of digital transformation. By comprehending AWS, Azure, and GCP, staying updated with industry trends, and actively participating in the cloud community, you'll not only optimize business operations but also contribute to the evolution of cloud computing solutions.

19

Unlocking the Potential of IoT

Unlocking the Potential of IoT: Programming for Seamless Integration of Physical and Digital Realms

1. Introduction to IoT:

- Definition:

IoT refers to the interconnected network of physical devices embedded with sensors, software, and connectivity for exchanging data.

-Scope:

Encompasses a wide range of applications, from smart homes to industrial automation.

2. Key Components of IoT:

-Devices and Sensors:

Physical components capturing data.

- Connectivity:

Networks facilitating data transfer.

-Cloud Computing:

Processing and storage of IoT data.

3. Programming Languages for IoT:

- C: Ideal for resource-constrained devices.

- Python:

Versatile language for IoT applications.

-Java:

Platform-independent language suitable for diverse devices.

4. IoT Development Platforms:

- Arduino:

Beginner-friendly platform for prototyping.

-Raspberry Pi:

Versatile platform supporting various programming languages.

-ESP8266/ESP32:

Low-cost platforms for IoT projects.

5. IoT Communication Protocols:

-MQTT (Message Queuing Telemetry Transport):

Lightweight and efficient for sensor networks.

- CoAP (Constrained Application Protocol):

Designed for resource-constrained devices.

- HTTP/HTTPS:

Common protocols for web-based communication.

6. Sensor Integration:

-Interfacing Sensors:

Connect and read data from sensors.

-Analog and Digital Sensors:

Understand the difference and usage.

7. Data Processing in IoT:

-Edge Computing:

Process data closer to the source for reduced latency.

-Cloud-Based Processing:

Utilize cloud platforms for intensive data analysis.

8. IoT Security Best Practices:

-Device Authentication:

Secure devices through authentication mechanisms.

-Data Encryption:

Encrypt data during transmission.

- Firmware Updates:

Implement secure methods for updating device firmware.

9. IoT Connectivity Options:

-Wi-Fi:

Common for home-based IoT devices.

- Bluetooth:

Suitable for short-range communication.

- LoRaWAN:

Long-range, low-power communication for IoT networks.

10. IoT Application Development:

-Mobile Apps:

Develop apps for remote device control.

- Web Interfaces:

Create web-based dashboards for monitoring.

11. IoT and Machine Learning Integration:

- Predictive Maintenance:

Use ML for predicting device failures.

-Anomaly Detection:

Identify abnormal patterns in IoT data.

12. IoT in Industry 4.0:

-Smart Manufacturing:

Implement automation and data exchange in manufacturing.

- Supply Chain Optimization:

Track and optimize the supply chain with IoT.

13. IoT and Edge AI:

-Edge AI Applications:

Deploy AI models on edge devices for real-time processing.

-TensorFlow Lite and ONNX:

Frameworks for running AI models on edge devices.

14. IoT Prototyping and Development Tools:

-PlatformIO:

Integrated development environment for IoT.

- Node-RED:

Visual tool for wiring IoT devices.

15. IoT Standards and Frameworks:

- IoTivity:

Open-source framework for IoT.

- OneM2M:

Standardizing communication between IoT devices.

16. IoT and Cloud Integration:

-AWS IoT Core:

AWS service for managing IoT devices.

- Azure IoT Hub:

Microsoft's platform for IoT device management.

17. IoT Data Visualization:

- Grafana and Kibana:

Tools for creating dashboards and visualizing IoT data.

- Custom Dashboards:

Design user-friendly interfaces for data representation.

18. IoT Ethics and Privacy:

- Data Ownership:

Clarify ownership and usage of collected data.

- User Consent:

Ensure users are informed and consent to data collection.

19. Continuous Learning and Community Engagement:

-IoT Conferences and Meetups:

Stay updated with the latest trends and technologies.

-IoT Forums:

Engage with the IoT community for knowledge sharing.

20. Contributing to Open Source IoT Projects:

-GitHub Contributions:

Collaborate on open-source IoT projects.

- Knowledge Sharing:

Contribute to documentation and community forums.

Conclusion:

Programming for IoT opens doors to a realm where the physical and digital seamlessly converge. By mastering languages, platforms, and standards, and actively engaging with the IoT community, you'll not only create innovative solutions but also contribute to the evolution of this transformative technology.

20

Mastering Automation Scripting

Mastering Automation Scripting: Streamlining Tasks with Bash and PowerShell

1. Introduction to Automation Scripting:

- Definition:

Automation scripting involves using scripting languages to automate repetitive tasks and processes.

- Purpose:

Enhance efficiency, reduce manual effort, and ensure consistency in workflows.

2. Choosing the Right Scripting Language:

- Bash:

Common on Unix-based systems (Linux, macOS).

- PowerShell:

Native to Windows environments.

3. Getting Started with Bash:

-Basics of Shell Scripting:

Understanding commands, variables, and control structures.

- Shebang (#!/bin/bash):

Indicating the interpreter for the script.

4. Essentials of PowerShell:

-Cmdlets and Pipelines:

Leveraging built-in commands and chaining them.

-Script Execution Policies:

Configuring policies for running PowerShell scripts.

5. Common Automation Tasks:

-File Operations:

Copying, moving, and deleting files.

-Directory Navigation:

Navigating and manipulating directories.

6. Working with Variables:

-Variable Declaration:

Assigning values to variables.

-Data Types:

Understanding string, integer, and array variables.

7. Conditional Statements:

-Bash `if` Statements:

Implementing conditional logic.

-PowerShell `if` Statements:

Executing actions based on conditions.

8. Loops and Iterations:

-Bash `for` and `while` Loops:

Iterating through sequences or based on conditions.

-PowerShell `foreach` and `while` Loops:

Looping constructs for different scenarios.

9. Functions and Modularization:

-Defining Functions in Bash:

Creating reusable code blocks.

-PowerShell Functions:

Structuring code into functions for maintainability.

10. Handling Input and Output:

-Bash Input and Output Redirection:

Redirecting standard input and output.

-PowerShell Output Formatting:

Formatting and presenting output.

11. Error Handling:

-Bash Error Handling:

Managing errors in scripts.

-PowerShell Try-Catch Blocks:

Handling exceptions in PowerShell.

12. Interacting with the System:

-Running System Commands (Bash):

Executing external commands within scripts.

-PowerShell System Management:

Utilizing PowerShell for system administration.

13. Working with Remote Systems:

-SSH and Remote Execution (Bash):

Running scripts on remote servers.

- PowerShell Remoting:

Remotely managing Windows machines.

14. Scheduled Tasks and Cron Jobs:

- Cron Jobs (Bash):

Scheduling recurring tasks in Unix environments.

-Task Scheduler (PowerShell):

Automating tasks on Windows using Task Scheduler.

15. Automation in Networking:

-Network Configuration (Bash):

Automating network-related tasks.

-PowerShell Networking Cmdlets:

Managing network settings in Windows.

16. Working with APIs:

- cURL and API Calls (Bash):

Making HTTP requests from the command line.

-Invoke-RestMethod (PowerShell):

Interacting with REST APIs in PowerShell.

17. Scripting Best Practices:

-Documentation:

Commenting and documenting code for clarity.

-Error Handling Strategies:

Implementing effective error handling.

18. Version Control for Scripts:

-Git Integration:

Tracking changes and collaborating on scripts.

-GitHub and PowerShell Module Development:

Developing and sharing PowerShell modules.

19. Security Considerations:

Secure Script Execution:

Setting execution policies and securing scripts.

- Credential Handling (PowerShell):

Safely managing credentials in PowerShell scripts.

20. Continuous Learning and Community Engagement:

-Online Resources:

Exploring tutorials, forums, and documentation.

-Scripting Communities:

Engaging with scripting communities for knowledge exchange.

Conclusion:

Automation scripting is a powerful tool for simplifying and streamlining tasks.

By mastering Bash and PowerShell, adopting best practices, and actively participating in the scripting community, you'll not only optimize workflows but also contribute to the efficiency and reliability of systems and processes.

21

Mastering CI/CD

Mastering CI/CD: Automating Code Testing and Deployment for Seamless Development Workflows

1. Introduction to CI/CD:

- Definition:

Continuous Integration (CI) and Continuous Deployment (CD) are software development practices that automate the testing and deployment of code changes.

- Objectives:

Enhance collaboration, detect issues early, and deliver software faster.

2. Key Concepts:

-Continuous Integration (CI):

Integration of code changes into a shared repository multiple times a day.

- Continuous Deployment (CD):

Automated release of code to production after passing CI tests.

3. CI/CD Tools:

- Jenkins:

Open-source automation server supporting building, testing, and deployment.

- GitLab CI/CD:

Integrated CI/CD within the GitLab repository.

- Travis CI:

Cloud-based CI/CD service.

4. Version Control Integration:

-Git Integration:

Utilizing version control systems like Git for tracking changes.

- Branching Strategies:

Adopting effective branching models for CI/CD.

5. Setting Up CI:

-Automated Builds:

Configuring tools like Jenkins to automatically build code.

-Unit Testing:

Implementing automated unit tests in the CI process.

6. Artifact Management:

-Artifact Repositories:

Storing and managing build artifacts.

-Dependency Management:

Handling project dependencies in CI.

7. Static Code Analysis:

-Code Quality Tools:

Integrating tools like SonarQube for static code analysis.

- Linting:

Enforcing coding standards through automated linting.

8. Automated Testing:

- Unit Tests:

Ensuring individual components work as intended.

- Integration Tests:

Verifying interactions between components.

9. Code Coverage:

- Test Coverage Metrics:

Measuring the percentage of code covered by tests.

- Improving Code Coverage:

Strategies to enhance test coverage.

10. Continuous Deployment:

-Deployment Pipelines:

Defining automated pipelines for deploying code changes.

-Rolling Deployments:

Gradual deployment strategies for minimizing impact.

11. Infrastructure as Code (IaC):

- Configuration Management:

Using tools like Ansible, Chef, or Puppet for IaC.

-Immutable Infrastructure:

Treating infrastructure as code to ensure consistency.

12. Containerization and Orchestration:

-Docker:

Containerizing applications for consistency across environments.

-Kubernetes:

Orchestrating and managing containerized applications.

13. Monitoring and Logging:

-CI/CD Metrics:

Monitoring the performance of CI/CD pipelines.

-Logging Strategies:

Effective logging for troubleshooting.

14. Rollback Strategies:

-Automated Rollback:

Implementing automated rollback mechanisms.

-Manual Intervention:

Allowing manual intervention in specific cases.

15. Security in CI/CD:

-Static Application Security Testing (SAST):

Scanning code for security vulnerabilities.

-Dependency Scanning:

Checking dependencies for security issues.

16. Environment Management:

-Multiple Environments:

Configuring different environments (development, staging, production).

-Environment Variables:

Managing environment-specific configurations.

17. Collaboration and Code Review:

- Pull Requests:

Integrating code review into the CI/CD workflow.

-Automated Code Review Tools:

Enhancing code quality through automated reviews.

18. Documentation:

- Pipeline Documentation:

Providing clear documentation for CI/CD pipelines.

-Release Notes Automation:

Automating the generation of release notes.

19. User Acceptance Testing (UAT):

- Automated UAT:

Streamlining user acceptance testing in CI/CD.

- Feedback Loops:

Gathering user feedback for continuous improvement.

20. Continuous Learning and Community Engagement:

-CI/CD Webinars and Conferences:

Staying updated with the latest practices and tools.

-Community Forums:

Engaging with the CI/CD community for knowledge sharing.

Conclusion:

Mastering CI/CD is pivotal in modern software development. By understanding the core concepts, implementing effective CI/CD pipelines, and actively participating in the CI/CD community, you'll not only streamline development workflows but also contribute to the agility and reliability of software delivery processes.

22

Mastering Agile Methodology

Mastering Agile Methodology: Navigating Efficient Project Management

1. Introduction to Agile:

- Definition:

Agile is an iterative and incremental approach to project management and product development that prioritizes flexibility and customer satisfaction.

Agile Manifesto:

Core values and principles emphasizing individuals, interactions, and customer collaboration.

2. Key Agile Methodologies:

-Scrum:

Framework emphasizing collaboration, accountability, and iterative progress.

- Kanban:

Visual management method focusing on continuous delivery.

- Extreme Programming (XP):

Emphasizes code quality, continuous testing, and rapid iterations.

3. Agile Roles and Responsibilities:

- Product Owner:

Represents customer needs and sets priorities.

- Scrum Master:

Facilitates the Scrum process and removes impediments.

- Development Team:

Cross-functional team members responsible for delivering increments.

4. Agile Ceremonies:

-Sprint Planning:

Collaborative session to plan upcoming work.

-Daily Standup (Scrum):

Brief daily meeting for team synchronization.

-Sprint Review:

Demo of completed work at the end of a sprint.

5. Agile Artifacts:

-Product Backlog:

Prioritized list of features and enhancements.

-Sprint Backlog:

Work selected from the product backlog for a specific sprint.

- Burndown Charts:

Visual representation of work completed versus work remaining.

6. User Stories and Epics:

-User Story Format:

As a [user], I want [action], so that [benefit].

- Epics:

Larger bodies of work broken down into manageable stories.

7. Agile Estimation Techniques:

- Story Points:

Relative estimation based on complexity.

- Planning Poker:

Collaborative estimation using cards.

8. Continuous Improvement:

- Retrospectives:

Regular team meetings to reflect on processes and identify improvements.

-Kaizen:

Continuous improvement philosophy to enhance efficiency.

9.Prioritization Techniques:

- MoSCoW Method:

Must-haves, Should-haves, Could-haves, and Won't-haves.

-Value-Based Prioritization:

Prioritize features based on business value.

10. Agile Metrics:

- Velocity:

Measure of the amount of work a team can complete in a sprint.

- Lead Time and Cycle Time:

Measure the time taken from idea to delivery.

11. Agile and Remote Work:

-Virtual Boards (Kanban):

Online tools for managing work.

-Daily Check-Ins:

Virtual standup meetings to maintain communication.

12. Scaling Agile:

-SAFe (Scaled Agile Framework):

Framework for scaling Agile to larger organizations.

-LeSS (Large Scale Scrum):

Scaling Scrum principles for larger teams.

13. Agile and DevOps Integration:

- Continuous Integration (CI):

Frequent automated code integration.

-Continuous Deployment (CD):

Automating the deployment process.

14. Agile in Different Industries:

- Agile in Software Development:

Iterative development and rapid delivery.

- Agile in Marketing:

Adaptation to changing market demands.

15. Agile Leadership:

-Servant Leadership:

Leaders support and empower their teams.

-Agile Mindset:

Embrace change and continuous learning.

16. Agile Certification and Training:

-Certified ScrumMaster (CSM):

Scrum-specific certification.

-PMI Agile Certified Practitioner (PMI-ACP):

Broad Agile certification covering multiple methodologies.

17. Agile Documentation:

-Working Software Over Comprehensive Documentation (Agile Manifesto):

Emphasis on delivering value over extensive documentation.

Minimal Viable Product (MVP):

Release of a product with minimum features for rapid feedback.

18. Agile in a Hybrid Environment:

- Waterfall and Agile Hybrid:

Integrating Agile practices in traditional project management.

- Agile-Friendly Tools:

Utilizing tools that support Agile methodologies.

19. Community Engagement and Networking:

-Agile Conferences and Meetups:

Attend events to stay updated with Agile trends.

-Agile Forums and Online Communities:

Engage with the Agile community for knowledge exchange.

20. Contributing to Agile Practices:

- Sharing Knowledge:

Contribute to Agile discussions and share insights.

- Mentoring:

Guide others in adopting Agile principles.

Conclusion:

Mastering Agile methodology involves embracing flexibility, collaboration, and continuous improvement.

By understanding Agile frameworks, practicing Agile principles, and actively participating in the Agile community, you'll not only enhance project management efficiency but also contribute to a culture of adaptability and innovation.

23

Mastering DevOps Practices

Mastering DevOps Practices: Bridging the Gap Between Development and Operations

1.Introduction to DevOps:

-Definition:

DevOps is a set of practices that aims to automate and improve the collaboration between software development (Dev) and IT operations (Ops).

- Key Objectives:

Accelerate delivery, improve reliability, and foster a culture of continuous feedback.

2. Core DevOps Principles:

-Automation:

Automate repetitive tasks to enhance efficiency.

-Collaboration:

Promote seamless communication and collaboration.

-Continuous Integration (CI):

Integrate code changes frequently to detect and address issues early.

- Continuous Deployment (CD):

Automate the deployment process for rapid and reliable releases.

-Monitoring and Feedback:

Implement monitoring to gather feedback and facilitate continuous improvement.

3. DevOps Culture:

-Collaborative Environment:

Foster a culture of collaboration and shared responsibility.

-Communication:

Break down silos and encourage open communication.

-Continuous Learning:

Embrace a mindset of continuous improvement and learning.

4. DevOps Practices:

- Infrastructure as Code (IaC):

Define and manage infrastructure through code.

- Version Control:

Use version control systems (e.g., Git) for tracking changes.

- Configuration Management:

Automate and manage configurations consistently.

5. Continuous Integration (CI):

-Automated Builds:

Automatically build and test code upon changes.

-Code Quality Checks:

Implement code quality checks as part of the CI process.

6. Continuous Deployment (CD):

-Automated Deployment:
    Automate the deployment process for faster releases.

- Rollback Strategies:

Implement automated rollback mechanisms for failed deployments.

7. Monitoring and Logging:

- Real-time Monitoring:

Monitor applications and infrastructure in real-time.

- Centralized Logging:

Aggregate logs for troubleshooting and analysis.

8. Collaborative Tools:

- Communication Platforms:

Utilize collaboration tools (e.g., Slack, Microsoft Teams) for real-time communication.

- Project Management Tools:

Choose tools that support collaboration and transparency.

9. Automated Testing:

-Unit Testing:

Automate unit tests for code quality assurance.

-Integration Testing:

Implement automated integration tests.

10. Security Practices:

- DevSecOps:

Integrate security practices into the DevOps pipeline.

-Automated Security Scans:

Implement automated security scans for vulnerabilities.

11. Containerization and Orchestration:

-Docker:

Containerize applications for consistency.

-Kubernetes:

Orchestrate and manage containerized applications.

12. Collaborative Documentation:

-Wiki and Documentation:

Maintain comprehensive and collaborative documentation.

-Runbooks:

Document procedures and operational processes.

13. Infrastructure Monitoring:

-Resource Utilization:

Monitor server and application resource utilization.

-Alerting Mechanisms:

Implement alerts for timely issue detection.

14.Incident Response and Resolution:

-Automated Incident Response:

Implement automated responses to common incidents.

-Post-Incident Analysis:

Conduct post-incident analysis for continuous improvement.

15. GitOps Practices:

-Declarative Configuration:

Use declarative configuration stored in Git repositories.

-Automated Synchronization:

Automate synchronization of configurations with the desired state.

16. Continuous Learning and Training:

- Training Programs:

Invest in continuous training for DevOps teams.

- Knowledge Sharing Sessions:

Facilitate knowledge-sharing sessions within the team.

17. DevOps Metrics:

-Lead Time and Cycle Time:

Measure the time from idea to production.

-Change Failure Rate:

Evaluate the success rate of changes.

18.DevOps in Different Environments:

-Cloud DevOps:

Utilize cloud services for scalable and flexible infrastructure.

- On-Premises DevOps:

Adapt DevOps practices for on-premises environments.

19. DevOps Tools and Ecosystem:

- CI/CD Tools:

Jenkins, GitLab CI, Travis CI.

-Infrastructure Tools:

Terraform, Ansible, Chef, Puppet.

-Monitoring Tools:

Prometheus, Grafana, ELK Stack.

20. Community Engagement and Contribution:

-DevOps Conferences and Meetups:

Attend events to stay updated with DevOps trends.

-Open Source Contributions:

Contribute to open-source DevOps projects.

Conclusion:

Mastering DevOps practices involves blending automation, collaboration, and continuous improvement. By embracing DevOps principles, implementing key practices, and actively engaging with the DevOps community, you'll not only streamline development and operations but also contribute to a culture of innovation and reliability.

24

Mastering APIs and Web Services

Mastering APIs and Web Services: Building Scalable and Interconnected Systems

1. Introduction to APIs:

-Definition:

LnAn Application Programming Interface (API) defines the interactions between software components, allowing them to communicate and share data.

-Types of APIs:

RESTful APIs, SOAP APIs, GraphQL, etc.

2. Understanding Web Services:

- Web Service Types:

RESTful Web Services and SOAP Web Services.

-REST (Representational State Transfer):

Architectural style emphasizing stateless communication.

-SOAP (Simple Object Access Protocol):

Protocol for exchanging structured information in web services.

3. RESTful API Design:

-Resource Identification:

Identifying resources with URIs.

-HTTP Methods:

Utilizing GET, POST, PUT, DELETE for CRUD operations.

-Stateless Communication:

Stateless nature of RESTful interactions.

4. RESTful API Endpoints:

-Resource Endpoints:

Defining endpoints for resources (e.g., /users, /products).

-Query Parameters:

Using parameters for data filtering and pagination.

5. HTTP Status Codes:

-Common Status Codes:

200 OK, 201 Created, 400 Bad Request, 404 Not Found, etc.

-Status Code Selection:

Choosing appropriate status codes for API responses.

6. Authentication and Authorization:

-API Keys:

Using API keys for authentication.

-OAuth 2.0:

Authentication framework for secure API access.

7. Data Formats:

-JSON (JavaScript Object Notation):

Lightweight and widely used for data exchange.

-XML (eXtensible Markup Language):

Used in SOAP-based APIs.

8. API Documentation:

-Swagger/OpenAPI Specification:

Documenting APIs for developers.

- Interactive Documentation Tools:

Tools like Swagger UI for exploring and testing APIs.

9. Consuming RESTful APIs:

HTTP Requests:

Using libraries like Axios or Fetch for making HTTP requests.

-Handling Responses:

Parsing JSON responses and error handling.

10.RESTful API Best Practices:

-Versioning:

Implementing versioning for API changes.

-Consistent Naming Conventions:

Adopting clear and consistent naming conventions.

11. SOAP Web Services

-XML-based Messaging:

Structuring data in XML format.

-WSDL (Web Services Description Language):

Defining the interface and operations.

12. Creating SOAP Web Services:

-Implementing Endpoints:

Developing endpoints for SOAP operations.

- WS-Security:

Adding security features to SOAP services.

13. API Testing:

-Unit Testing:

Testing individual components of the API.

-Integration Testing:

Verifying interactions between different components.

14. Webhooks:

-Definition:

Mechanism for real-time communication between systems.

-Implementing Webhooks:

Setting up endpoints to receive webhook events.

15. GraphQL:

-Query Language:

Efficiently fetching data with GraphQL queries.

-Mutation Operations:

Modifying data through GraphQL mutations.

16. API Security:

-HTTPS Usage:

Ensuring secure communication over HTTPS.

- Rate Limiting:

Implementing rate limiting to prevent abuse.

17. API Gateway:

-Definition:

Centralized entry point for managing and securing APIs.

-Benefits of API Gateway:

Load balancing, security, rate limiting, and analytics.

18. Microservices Architecture:

-APIs in Microservices:

Communication between microservices through APIs.

-Decentralized Data Management:

Each microservice manages its data through APIs.

19. API Monitoring and Analytics:

-Logging and Auditing:

Monitoring API usage and logging events.

-Analytics Tools:

Utilizing analytics tools for insights into API performance.

20. Community Engagement and Contribution:

-API Developer Communities:

Engaging with API communities for knowledge exchange.

-Contributing to Open Source APIs:

Contributing to open-source API projects.

Conclusion:

Mastering APIs and web services is essential for building scalable and interconnected systems.

By understanding the principles of RESTful APIs, SOAP services, GraphQL, and embracing best practices, you'll not only create efficient APIs but also contribute to the seamless integration of software components.

25

Mastering UI/UX Principles

Mastering UI/UX Principles: Crafting User-Friendly Applications

1. Introduction to UI/UX:

-Definition:

User Interface (UI) focuses on the visual aspects of an application, while User Experience (UX) encompasses the overall feel and usability.

-Key Objectives:

Enhance user satisfaction, accessibility, and overall usability.

2. UI Design Principles:

- Consistency:

Maintain a uniform design throughout the application.

-Hierarchy:

Organize elements to guide users through information.

-Feedback:

Provide visual and interactive feedback for user actions.

3. Color Theory in UI Design:

-Color Psychology:

Understand the emotional impact of colors.

-Contrast and Readability:

Ensure text and elements are easily readable.

4. Typography and Font Selection:

-Readability:

Choose fonts that are easy to read on various devices.

-Hierarchy with Fonts:

Use font sizes and weights for hierarchy.

5.UI Elements and Components:

-Buttons and Calls to Action:

Design intuitive buttons for clear calls to action.

-Forms and Input Fields:

Streamline form design for ease of input.

6.Responsive Design:

-Adaptability:

Ensure the interface works seamlessly across devices.

-Mobile-First Approach:

Prioritize design for mobile devices.

7. Microinteractions:

-Subtle Animations:

Use microinteractions for a delightful user experience.

-Feedback and Confirmation:

Visualize user actions with subtle animations.

8. UX Research and User Personas:

-User Personas:

Create detailed profiles of target users.

-User Journeys:

Map out the user's experience from entry to completion.

9. Wireframing and Prototyping:

-Wireframing Tools:

Use tools like Sketch, Figma, or Adobe XD.

Interactive Prototypes:

Create prototypes for user testing and feedback.

10.Usability Testing:

-Testing Scenarios:

Define specific tasks for users to complete.

-Feedback Collection:

Gather user feedback on the application's usability.

11. Accessibility in UI/UX:

-WCAG Guidelines:

Comply with Web Content Accessibility Guidelines.

-Alt Text for Images:

Provide alternative text for images.

12. UI/UX and Branding:

-Consistent Branding Elements:

Reflect brand identity in UI elements.

-Visual Language:

Develop a visual language that aligns with brand guidelines.

13. UI/UX in E-commerce:

-Clear Navigation:

Simplify product discovery and checkout processes.

-Trust Indicators:

Build trust with secure payment options and reviews.

14. UI/UX in Mobile Apps:

Intuitive Navigation:

Optimize navigation for smaller screens.

-Gestures and Interactions:

Leverage mobile gestures for smooth interactions.

15.UI/UX Trends and Innovation:

-Dark Mode:

Offer a dark mode option for reduced eye strain.

-3D Elements:

Integrate subtle 3D design elements.

16. UI/UX Collaboration with Development:

- Design Systems:

Create design systems for consistent development.

- Collaborative Tools:

Foster communication between designers and developers.

17. UI Copywriting:

-Clarity and Conciseness:

Craft clear and concise UI text.

-Microcopy:

Use microcopy for helpful hints and instructions.

18. Continuous UI/UX Improvement:

-User Feedback Loops:

Collect and analyze user feedback regularly.

-A/B Testing:

Test variations to optimize user interactions.

19. Community Engagement and Networking:

-UI/UX Meetups and Conferences:

Attend events to stay updated with industry trends.

-Online Forums and Communities:

Engage with UI/UX communities for knowledge sharing.

20. Contributing to Open Source UI/UX:

-Open Source Design Projects:

Contribute to open-source UI/UX projects.

-Sharing Insights:

Share UI/UX insights through blogs or presentations.

Conclusion:

Mastering UI/UX principles involves combining aesthetics with usability. By understanding design principles, conducting thorough research, and embracing continuous improvement, you'll not only create visually appealing interfaces but also provide users with a seamless and enjoyable experience.

26

Mastering Code Reviews

Mastering Code Reviews: Elevating Code Quality through Collaboration

1. Introduction to Code Reviews:

-Purpose:

Code reviews are a collaborative process where team members evaluate code changes to ensure quality, identify issues, and share knowledge.

-Key Objectives:

Enhance code quality, promote best practices, and facilitate learning within the team.

2. The Importance of Code Reviews:

- Quality Assurance:

Detect and rectify bugs, ensuring a robust codebase.

-Knowledge Sharing:

Exchange ideas, techniques, and best practices.

3. Roles in Code Reviews:

- Author:

Developer who wrote the code changes.

-Reviewer:

Team member(s) responsible for evaluating the code.

4. Code Review Workflow:

-Initiation:

Code author submits changes for review.

-Review:

Reviewers examine the code for issues and improvements.

-Discussion:

Collaborative discussion between author and reviewers.

-Approval or Iteration:

Code is approved or requires further refinement.

5. Code Review Best Practices:

-Clear Objectives:

Define the purpose and expectations of the code review.

-Small, Digestible Changes:

Break down changes into manageable units for effective review.

6. Setting Up Code Review Guidelines:

-Coding Standards:

Establish and enforce coding standards for consistency.

-Checklists:

Provide checklists to ensure comprehensive reviews.

7. Effective Code Review Comments:

-Constructive Feedback:

Frame comments positively and suggest improvements.

-Specificity:

Provide detailed feedback for better understanding.

8. Code Review Tools:

-Version Control Platforms:

Leverage tools like GitHub, GitLab, or Bitbucket.

-Code Review Platforms:

Utilize dedicated tools such as Crucible or Gerrit.

9. Automated Code Review:

-Linting and Static Analysis:

Implement tools for automated code analysis.

-Continuous Integration Integration:

Integrate code reviews into CI/CD pipelines.

10.Code Review Etiquette:

-Respectful Communication:

Maintain a respectful and positive tone in comments.

-Timeliness:

Strive for timely reviews to prevent bottlenecks.

11. Learning from Code Reviews:

-Reviewing Others' Code:

Learn different approaches and techniques.

-Accepting Feedback:

Embrace feedback as an opportunity for growth.

12. Code Review Metrics:

-Review Velocity:

Measure the time taken to complete code reviews.

-Review Coverage:

Ensure fair distribution of reviews among team members.

13. Continuous Improvement:

-Retrospectives:

Conduct regular retrospectives to refine the code review process.

-Feedback Loops:

Gather feedback on the effectiveness of code reviews.

14.Handling Disagreements:

-Open Dialogue:

Encourage open communication to resolve disagreements.

-Seeking Consensus:

Work collaboratively to reach consensus on issues.

15. Remote Code Reviews:

-Collaborative Tools:

Utilize video calls or collaborative platforms for remote reviews.

-Clear Documentation:

Provide comprehensive documentation for remote reviewers.

16. Code Review and Team Collaboration:

-Cross-Functional Reviews:

Encourage reviews by members with different expertise.

-Knowledge Transfer:

Use code reviews as an opportunity for knowledge exchange.

17. Senior Developer Involvement:

-Mentoring through Reviews:

Senior developers can mentor through code reviews.

-Leading by Example:

Set high standards through exemplary code reviews.

18. Code Review in Agile Development:

-Integration with Sprints:

Integrate code reviews into the sprint cycle.

-Iterative Refinement:

Continuously refine code based on feedback.

19. Community Engagement and Best Practices:

- Participate in Code Review Communities:

Engage with online communities for code review best practices.

-Contribute to Open Source Reviews:

Contribute to open-source projects to enhance your reviewing skills.

20.Encouraging a Positive Code Review Culture:

-Celebrating Success:

Acknowledge and celebrate well-executed code reviews.

-Continuous Learning:

Foster a culture of continuous learning and improvement.

Conclusion:

Mastering code reviews is an integral part of collaborative software development.

By embracing effective practices, cultivating a positive review culture, and learning from each iteration, teams can consistently enhance their code quality, promote knowledge sharing, and foster a culture of continuous improvement.

<h1 style="text-align:center">27</h1>

Mastering Documentation Skills

Mastering Documentation Skills: Enhancing Code Comprehension and Collaboration

1. Introduction to Documentation Skills:

-Purpose:

Documentation is a crucial aspect of software development that aims to provide clarity, context, and understanding of code for developers, users, and collaborators.

-Key Objectives:

Facilitate comprehension, streamline collaboration, and ensure the sustainability of code.

2. Types of Documentation:

-Code Comments:

In-line comments explaining code logic and functionality.

-README Files:

Overview of the project, setup instructions, and basic usage.

-API Documentation:

Detailed documentation for functions, classes, and APIs.

3. Benefits of Good Documentation:

-Improved Understanding:

Enhance code comprehension for developers.

-Onboarding Efficiency:

Facilitate quicker onboarding of new team members.

4. Code Comments Best Practices:

-Purposeful Comments:

Provide comments where the code might be non-intuitive.

-Avoid Redundancy:

Ensure comments add value and don't duplicate code.

5. README Files:

-Project Overview:

Concise explanation of the project's purpose and goals.

-Installation Instructions:

Step-by-step guide for setting up the project.

-Usage Examples:

Demonstrations of how to use the project.

6.API Documentation:

-Method/Function Descriptions:

Detailing parameters, return values, and usage examples.

-Endpoint Information:

For web APIs, document available endpoints and their functionalities.

7. Documentation Tools:

-Documentation Generators:

Utilize tools like Javadoc, Doxygen, or Sphinx.

-Markdown:

Create clear and formatted documentation using Markdown.

8. Writing Clear and Concise Documentation:

-Avoid Jargon:

Write for an audience with varied expertise.

-Visual Aids:

Use diagrams or charts for complex concepts.

9. Updating Documentation:

-Version Control:

Keep documentation in sync with code changes using version control.

-Changelogs:

Maintain a changelog to track modifications.

10. Documentation Standards:

-Consistent Style:

Adopt a consistent writing style across documentation.

-Template Usage:

Develop and adhere to a documentation template.

11. Collaborative Documentation:

-Wikis:

Utilize collaborative platforms for team wikis.

-Feedback Mechanisms:

Encourage team members to provide feedback.

12. Documentation as a Learning Tool:

-Educational Content:

Use documentation to educate team members on project intricacies.

-Tutorials and Guides:

Include tutorials and guides for complex features.

13. User-Friendly Documentation:

-Searchable Content:

Make documentation easily searchable.

-Table of Contents:

Include a clear table of contents for navigation.

14. Documenting Code Patterns:

-Design Patterns:

Explain the use of design patterns in your codebase.

-Coding Conventions:

Document and adhere to coding conventions.

15. Documentation Review:

-Peer Review:

Include documentation review as part of the code review process.

-Feedback Integration:

Act on feedback received during documentation reviews.

16. Documenting Bug Fixes and Issues:

-Bug Reports:

Detail steps to reproduce, affected versions, and resolutions.

-Issue Templates:

Use templates for consistent issue documentation.

17. Documentation Maintenance:

-Regular Updates:

Schedule regular updates to reflect code changes.

-Retirement Plans:

Document procedures for retiring features or code.

18.Documentation in Agile Development:

User Stories:

Include documentation tasks in user stories.

Incremental Documentation:

Document features incrementally as they are developed.

19. Community Engagement and Best Practices:

-Documentation Workshops:

Organize workshops for improving documentation skills.

-Contributing to Open Source Documentation:

Contribute to open-source projects to enhance documentation skills.

20. Encouraging Documentation Ownership:

-Team Responsibilities:

Assign specific team members as documentation owners.

- Recognition:

Acknowledge and celebrate excellent documentation efforts.

Conclusion:

Mastering documentation skills is pivotal for fostering collaboration, ensuring code understanding, and maintaining a sustainable codebase.

By adhering to best practices, utilizing effective tools, and promoting a culture of documentation ownership, developers contribute to the longevity and success of software projects.

www.ingramcontent.com/pod-product-compliance
Lightning Source LLC
Chambersburg PA
CBHW070930260726
48661CB00003B/913